Sarah

By

Graham Field

Explanation.

The vast majority of this book is a commentary on the verses of scripture that refer to Sarah, and as such are my own work. I have used the New King James version and the New Living Translation as my primary references. Any correspondence with the works of other writers is simply due to the fact we have reached the same conclusions. I have explained that I have used as a basic premise, *'that to tell the story of Sarah, we must, at the same time, tell the story of Abraham.'* I have shown that I believe that Sarah was as much called of God as Abraham was.

I began this work by reading every verse in the Bible that mentions Sarah or Sarai, either directly or indirectly. From this I constructed the collage that forms the core material. I have illustrated the material by quoting from the Jewish Midrash as found in the Talmud, obtainable at various online sites. I have used other verses of scripture, which suggest a similar theme, to illustrate the commentary. Background material has been composed from various archaeological presentations from my own research. All works that have been quoted are acknowledged in the footnotes.

Contents

1. An Encounter with God in Ur.   1

2. Entering Canaan   17

3. Sarah: the woman.   33

4. Sarah's message to the people of faith.   56

5. The God of Abraham and Sarah.   74

6. Sarah: our mother.   95

7. Sarah's Legacy.   112

Sarah

Introduction.

The story of Sarah is set around 3 800 years ago. This means that many of the virtues we hold as an essential part of our Christian Heritage were not implemented. This does not mean that humanity was advancing on a journey of moral discovery, but that God's original ideal had become corrupted. In fact, the teachings of Jesus were based on this understanding. Jesus said that the moral standard we regard as Christian was the standard at the beginning but had been abandoned by the time of Sarah and Abraham. (Matthew 19: 8)

The story is built around such reprehensible things as slavery, bigamy, polygamy, trafficking, racism and male superiority. We are to understand that in no way is the Bible promoting these things, and we cannot excuse any conduct on this basis. What the text is saying to us is that God meets people where they are, Sarah in her day - ourselves in our day. Unless we tell the story as it is written we cannot hear the message that comes down through time to us.

This entire book was inspired by studying Galatians 4: 21-31, particularly the rendering in the New Living Translation, ' Sarah represents the free woman, and she is our mother.' All translations do not spell it out in this way, but however the text is translated the identity of Sarah is obvious..

It seems the Bible is giving the impression that Sarah, wife of Abraham, was only spoken of because it was necessary to explain the story. But I discovered that as one digs a little deeper in to the text and the Hebrew commentaries on the text, Sarah emerges as a woman of God in her own right. Sarah was as much called of God as Abraham was!

I was intrigued to see that Paul, in seeking to differentiate between law and grace; spiritual bondage and spiritual freedom; tradition and a dynamic faith; that which is eternal and that which is temporal, chose Sarah as the positive, supreme example.

Peter also regards Sarah as a role model. 1 Peter 3; 5-6. And the writer of the book of Hebrews regards her as a person of incredible personal faith

I decided I needed to find out who Sarah was and why Paul elevated her to such a prominent position as the mother of the people of faith.. The result is this book.

1

An Encounter with God in Ur.

This is the story of the life, times and faith of the most-mentioned woman in the bible. Owing to the dominance of the masculine gender in older English translations, in the stories regarding women, they tended to be eclipsed by their male counterparts and companions. Christian commentators, historically, follow this line when speaking of Sarah. Though never disrespected, she is often placed in the shadow of Abraham, who is depicted, quite rightly, as the great man of faith. Jewish commentators, however, see her rather differently. To them she is a star that shines in her own light in the story of World Redemption, and stands alongside, not in the shadow of, her husband in the journey they were called to undertake.

> *Look to Abraham your father **and** to Sarah who bore you; for I called him alone and blessed him and increased him. Isaiah 51: 2*

Although Abraham experienced the initial encounter with God, he could not fulfil his calling without Sarah, in this sense he was '*increased.*' In this book I intend to present a picture of Sarah that shows that she was as much called of God as Abraham was, and contributed in equal measure, an example of the life of faith we are also called upon to follow. She was not just any woman, and as we shall see, no other woman could take her place, although they tried. Sarah was only the second woman in the Bible we know anything about, the first being Eve. Eve partnered with Adam and brought about devastation for the world, Sarah partnered with Abraham and brought about blessings for the world.

This establishes the fact that we cannot tell the story of Sarah without telling the story of Abraham, they were intertwined throughout their lives. The stories of the Patriarchs and Matriarchs of Israel are written in such a way that their experiences pre-figure, relate in cameo, or even predict, events in the journey of their descendants.

'Everything written in connection with our Father Abraham, is written in connection with his children.'[1]

The city of Ur.

We know a tremendous amount about this ancient region as over 500,000 clay tablets have been discovered and are preserved in museums around the world. The British museum is host to over 130,000 items. The language was Sumerian[2] and the writing called cuneiform.[3] The writing system was deciphered in the early 19th century and so the recorded information could be understood.

Abraham and Sarah were born and raised in the city of Ur, the remains of which is a site in modern day Iraq, covering about 50 to 60 acres. At the time, the city of Ur was one of the largest cities in the world, equivalent to today's Paris, London or New York.. It shared economic dominance of the region along with other ancient cities such as, Damascus, Jaffa, Tyre, Aleppo, Nineveh, Babylon and Jericho. It was situated at the extreme south-eastern edge of what became known as the Fertile Crescent. This was an arc of fertile land that stretched northwards from the Persian gulf between the rivers Tigris and Euphrates, sweeping through Syria and eastern

---

[1] Jewish Talmud, Genesis Rabbah 40:6.

[2] Named after the overall empire of the region of Sumar, Mesopotamia.

[3] The method of wring with wedge shaped stylus impressed into soft clay.

Turkey, and then moving south-west to incorporate the coastal cities of Lebanon and Israel.

The area between the two rivers, where Ur was situated, became known as Mesopotamia. (meaning between the rivers) and at the time was included in the Sumerian empire. It was so fertile that some have identified it as the Biblical Eden.[4] The biblical text sometimes called it 'Ur of the Chaldeans'[5] but that was a literary insertion by scribes to identify the place to their generations.

Ur and the surrounding area were at a watershed moment of human development. It is noted for the following;

- The earliest known record of the use of the wheel.
- It was one of the first places with a structured education system.
- The first manufacture of clay building bricks.
- The first language that could be both spoken and written with symbols for sounds.
- The first attempt to map the stars and designate the constellations.
- The first systems of mathematical accounting.[6]

Ur had been an ancient port settlement from time immemorial, but it took on its city status from around

---

[4] Genesis 2:14.

[5] The Chaldeans conquered Babylon in the 8th century BC.

[6] The Oxford Handbook of Science and Medicine in the Classical World.

3800 B.C. Although very old, it is dwarfed into insignificance by the dates that archaeology has proposed for the northern Mesopotamian cities of Catal Huyuk which it is claimed flourished between 7400 – 6400 B.C. And Gobekli Tepe which is claimed to have flourished between 9600 – 8200 B.C.

The cities of Mesopotamia have been called the 'cradle of civilization.'[7] Without any disrespect to any ethnic group, civilization has been defined as having evidence of the following:

- A farming industry that bred animals and produce surplus to requirement.
- Large settled concentrations of people in an urban area.
- A system of law and order.
- Defined boundaries of administration.
- A common written language and a system of education.
- An established system of commodity exchange.
- A clearly defined strata of society and division of labour.
- A devotion to religion, art and culture.[8]

Ur met all aspects of this criteria, and more, with flying colours. The evidence found in excavations show that Ur was an extremely affluent place to live. The inner city was built on elevated ground and

---

[7] The Fertile Crescent. National Geographic Society.
[8] Civilization. National Geographic Society

surrounded by wall reaching up to 8 metres in height. Everything was built of mud bricks as stone was not plentiful in the area. Within these walls, buildings were tightly packed together with little space between one building and the next.. Access was obtained through narrow winding streets. However, it was not as tightly packed as Catal Huyuk where the buildings were only accessible from the roof! There was an outer city, beyond the walls, where the buildings were larger and more elaborate. The entire area was surrounded, by the river Euphrates on the east, and man-made canals on the north, south, and west.

The population was divided into classes: Royalty and nobility; Priests; merchants and administrators; and servants slaves. However both men and women could rise through the classes by means of education, especially being able to read and write, and notable achievements.

The city was abandoned in the 5th century B.C. because of falling sea levels and the river Euphrates changing course.[9]

The religion of Ur.

We are particularly interested in the religion in Mesopotamia. Religion in the ancient world was not a matter of choice. The rulers of cities were often deified and the priests made sure everyone followed the rituals. Not to participate in the religion was seen as disloyalty and dissention and was dealt with

---

[9] World History Encyclopedia.

harshly. There were several temple sites within Ur. We must understand the idol temples were centres of the community. They were not, only places of worship but provided a place to eat, doctors surgeries, administration offices, recreation and, most importantly, schools. Refusal to worship the idols would also mean that you could be deprived the use of these other benefits.

There were many gods but the principal deity was the Moon God, Nanna, interestingly, with the crescent moon as an important symbol. The most prominent building in the city was a large Ziggurat. This was a pyramid-like structure where, unlike the Egyptian pyramids, the top was levelled off to create an elevated platform. This was the heart of religious practice and a place for the observation of the heavens. The more famous 'Tower of Babel', situated nearby, would also have been a Ziggurat. The Bible tells us that it was built to *'reach the heavens.'*[10] This of course, meant a place where the heavens could be observed and the movement of the stars and planets studied. This led to attempts to predict the future and manipulate the rhythm of life. The science of Astronomy, and the practice of Astrology both emerged from this region.

The reliance on astrology ensured that there was much superstition, represented by idols, which people worshipped, and who had counterparts in the cosmic constellations. These idols represented things that were essential to survival, such as; a rain god; a fertility god, a harvest god and so on. This

---

[10] Genesis 11: 1-9.

was the world into which Abraham and Sarah were born and raised. But much more of this later on.[11]

The Place of Women.

This of interest to us because it helps us to grasp something of who Sarah was and how she was raised.

Surprisingly, women like Sarah, had a significant amount of social autonomy. Technically they were the property of their husbands or fathers, but in practice they enjoyed a great deal of latitude. Women could divorce, own property, fill significant roles in society including the authority that went with that. Girls were not compelled to attend the temple-schools as the boys were, but they could be educated through private tuition. If they could read and write they could be involved as priestesses in the idol temples. At the lowest level of society women were slaves or prostitutes. It is fair to say, that the evidence that has survived, mostly describes women in the upper echelons of society.

We are aware when Sarah is introduced to us, the first personal thing we know about her that she was barren. It is interesting to see how Sarah would have been viewed in Ur. Barrenness was seen as a disability or abnormality opposed to the norm of fertility. The condition was seen as unfavourable disposition of the gods to the person so afflicted. This shows us that Sarah had a lot to deal with as a young woman in this environment.

---

[11] Encyclopedia Britannica; Wikipedia; Cambridge. Org. *et al.*

The Divine Encounter. [12]

> *El-ha Kavod[13] appeared to our father Abraham while he was in Mesopotamia, before he dwelt in Haran.[14] Acts 7: 2.*

The story begins in the household of Terah, the father of Abraham. Some manuscripts describe Terah as a priest, others a merchant. We are told how Terah descended from Noah through his son Shem. Abraham, known originally as Abram, had two brothers, Nahor and Haran. We are told that Haran had married, produced three children, but had tragically, already died, before the story of Abraham and Sarah begins. Nahor marries one of Haran's daughters, his niece, and moves away to a place that seems to have been named after his deceased brother, Haran. It was near to the ancient city we have mentioned, Gobekli Tepe. Abraham also marries a lady from within his family who seems to be known as Sarai, but much more about that later.

Somewhere in this milieu Abraham has this significant encounter with God. There are no records of any individual having a divine encounter with God since the days of Noah some 700 years previously, so this was a most remarkable occurrence.[15]

What actually happened to Abraham and Sarah in this encounter we do not know, except to say it radically changed everything they knew and

---

[12] Genesis 11: 27-32.

[13] The God of Glory.

[14] Haran is both the name of Abraham's brother and a place.

[15] Acts 7: 2-3.

believed up to that point. Terah was a worshipper of idols. Some rabbinical sources say that he was actually a manufacturer of idols.[16] As head of the clan, Terah would insist that all in his household worshipped as he did.

> And Joshua said to all the people, "Thus says the LORD God of Israel: 'Your fathers, including Terah, the father of Abraham and the father of Nahor, dwelt on the other side of the River in old times; and they served other gods. Joshua 24: 2.

There is an interesting story told in the Midrash as recorded in the Talmud.[17] One day Terah went on a journey and left Abram in charge of the business that sold idols.

---

[16] Genesis Rabbah 38: 13

[17] The Midrash was originally an oral commentary that accompanied the Torah. The original commentary, called the Mishnah, was not written down for centuries. It was believed to be a living commentary on the Torah. Eventually the record of what was passed on from generation to generation became far too large to be held in anyone's memory and so it was written down. It now became known as the 'Gemara,' or the completed Mishnah and formed the basis of the Talmud.

The Midrash is another section of the Talmud. The Talmud is a massive commentary on the Hebrew scriptures and seeks to describe how the Law applies to every area of life. All this material was assembled along with other commentaries and produced the Talmud, in 400 A.D. in Israel, and 500 A.D. in Babylon.

When a man would come to buy an idol, Abram would ask him: "How old are you?" The man would respond: "Fifty." Abram would reply: "Woe to this man, you are fifty years old and yet you bow to one who is only a day old!" The man would then feel embarrassed and slink away. One time a woman came carrying a dish of fine flour. She said to Abram: "Here, offer this before them." Abraham picked up a staff and broke the idols and placed the staff in the hands of the largest of them. When his father returned, he asked him: "Why did you do this to them?" Abraham replied: "Would I hide it from you? A woman came carrying a plate of fine flour and she told me to offer it before them. Each one of them said, 'I will eat first' until the largest of them picked up the staff and shattered the others." Terah responded: "Why are you trying to fool me? I know what they are!" Abraham retorted: "Do your ears not hear what your mouth is saying?!" [18]

Of course we have no means of verifying the story but it does sit easily with what we do know. As Abraham had experienced a Divine Encounter and as a result he had to negotiate the tricky matter of trying to persuade his father the reality of what had happened and why he no longer wished to serve idols. This was necessary because at the time Abraham could not make decisions without the blessing of his father. This would certainly be a good

---

[18] Genesis Rabbah 38. Rabbi Chiyya

way of doing it. He was successful up to a point because Terah did leave Ur.

Why did Terah leave Ur?

We don't know exactly why Terah left the comforts, security and prosperity of Ur, but he did leave with a destiny in mind: he set out, with his family, for Canaan. One reason why someone would make such a decision, would be to get away from something. The answer to what that could possibly be, is found in the Divine Encounter that Abraham had experienced. If Terah's family had turned their backs on idolatry then it would place them in a precarious position in Ur.

He must have, to some degree, believed Abraham, and was prepared to pay the price of a considerable social downgrade. We can see that such a move was no light matter. It appears to be an attempt to go back in time to a nomadic and simple lifestyle, away from the sophistication of the city. The advantage that it gave, was that Abraham could develop his belief in the One True God who had visited him, and teach others the same, without fear of reprisal from idol worshippers.

As it transpired Terah did not make it to Canaan (Israel) but settled in Haran, where Nahor had settled.[19] The city of Haran was still within the boundaries of Mesopotamia. There he lived out his days and was buried. Maybe the prospects of a

---

[19] Genesis 29:4

nomadic lifestyle became too much to contemplate at his age.

It seems that Terah was content to be beyond the influence of the idolatry of Ur, but not prepared to go all the way to Canaan. According to the life-spans mentioned in Genesis 11 it seems that Abraham stayed with Terah in Haran until he died.

> *Leave your country, from your family, and from your father's house.*[20]

Stephen refers to this when he said in Acts 7: 4:

> *Then he came out of the land of the Chaldeans and dwelt in Haran, And from there when his father was dead, He moved him to this land in which you now dwell.'*

Nahor, Abraham's brother, apparently, was not opposed to idol worship. His grandson, Laban was clearly an idol worshipper as can be seen when Rachel and Leah stole his gods. (Genesis 31: 19) We may assume that Terah's change of heart had to do with the lingering influence of idolatry, and his preference to stay with Nahor who had not taken on radical new religious views. As the only other reference to Terah in the Bible is to identify him as an idol worshipper, I think it is reasonable to conclude that Terah went half-heartedly. He had not experienced the Divine Encounter, and the whole thing was intriguing, but not as real to him, as it was to Abraham and Sarah.

---

[20] Genesis 12: 1-3,

An estimated timeline based on the Biblical data.

The following may be constructed from the Biblical evidence and likely conclusions.

- Terah was 205 when he died.
- Abraham was 75 and Sarah 65 when Terah died and they left the settlement of Haran for Canaan.
- Abraham and Sarah lived together in Canaan for 62 years.
- Therefore, Terah was 130 when Abraham was born and 140 when Sarah was born.
- Haran would have been about 60 when Abraham was born and about 70 when Sarah was born.
- Haran would have died between the ages of 70 and 100. He had to have died after Iscah was born and before Abraham and Sarah were married.
- If Abraham had married at the average age at the time, (Genesis 11:12-24) he would have been about 30 and Sarah about 20 when they were married.
- It would then mean they stayed in the settlement of Haran, with Terah, about 40-45 years.
- Abram and Sarah were married for about 107 years.
- Sarah was 127 when she died.
- Abraham was 137 when Sarah died and 175 when he died.
- It can be calculated from the Biblical text that Abraham was born in the 2,226[th] year after Adam was banished from the Garden of Eden.

- When Abraham was born Adam had been dead for about 1000 years; Noah about 200 years and Shem 100 years.

2

Entering Canaan

The land of Canaan.

The land of Canaan was named after Canaan, a grandson of Noah.[21] It is pronounced '*Cana'an.*' It eventually became an enormous area, far bigger than modern Israel, stretching to the banks of the Euphrates and including much of modern-day Syria, Jordan and Lebanon. (Genesis 15: 18-21) It was not a unified state, with borders and a capital city, as we understand nations today. It was a community of city-states, each with their own king, economy, laws

---

[21] Genesis 9: 15-20.

and religion, that acted independently. The narrative assumes that we know that. These ancient cities were built at the junctions of important trade routes, which usually meant, where valleys merged, or were ports on the coast. This arrangement was little different to the Canaan that Joshua discovered some 400/500 years later. (Numbers 13: 28-29; Deuteronomy 7: 1-5) To travel in this type of environment required some level of diplomacy and the ability to persuade people that your coming was of benefit to them.

However Canaan was not seen as a desirable place at this time by the Biblical authors. Genesis 9: 20-27 discreetly describes an act of sexual perversion by Ham with his father Noah, and as result, both he, and his inheritance are cursed. This understanding could have further contributed to Terah's decision to stop at Haran as he did not possess the burning calling of Abraham to enter the 'cursed' land. It seemed that a broad moral code emerged after the Flood which sought to avoid the wanton promiscuity that caused the Flood in the first place. Canaan did not hold to this moral code, and neither did he have any concept of the One True God. (Deuteronomy 18: 9-11) It seems, Terah decided that to enter Canaan was too high a price for him to pay, and that nothing good could come from it.

Also Canaan was an area that was continuously contested by the great powers of the time, mainly the Hittites and the Egyptians. It was strategic because it linked the ancient North African civilizations of Libya, Egypt and Ethiopia to the commercial centres of Mesopotamia. Whoever dominated Canaan could take of the rich pickings of North African and Mesopotamian trade. Because of this the city-states often changed hand during these conflicts.

Strangely Abraham and Sarah did not attempt to live in a city or try or found one in Canaan. It seems that the idea of city life could not be further from their minds. It is as if they saw something intrinsically evil in cities that would only work against their desire to serve the One True God.

> *By faith he dwelt in the land of promise as a stranger in a foreign country, dwelling in tents with Isaac and Jacob, the heirs with him of the same promise. For he waited for the city which has foundations, whose builder and maker is God. Hebrews 11: 9-10.*

The Divine Encounter had taught Abraham that it was not his calling to build anything that in anyway resembles Ur. He was convinced his calling was to sanctify the land, and prepare a people who would eventually form a nation, with the specific task of bringing about World Redemption. Abraham and Sarah had accumulated a large household of over 300 men, plus women and children.[22] We can expect that these people were taught the principle that drove them forwards, that of the revelation of the One True God. Later on, this revelation would be taught to Abraham and Sarah's descendants and their expanding progeny as neither Isaac nor Jacob had any interest in building anything except altars.[23]

---

[22] Genesis 14:14.

[23] Jacob did purchase the land on which he built his altar.

Eventually this progeny would be as numerous as the stars in heaven and the sand of the sea shore. This was to be *'the heavenly country.'* We need to take note, that when we look around us and see the moral and spiritual degeneracy of the age in which we live, that like Abraham and Sarah, we are only pilgrims here. This is not our final home. In other words, *'we are a people without a place.'* For centuries Jerusalem became a sacred place, but it was only a shadow of that which is to come. But we have come to realise that, like Abraham and Sarah, God was no less real to a person of faith, in one place or another. They could meet with God anywhere because God was everywhere. Jerusalem remains an absolutely fascinating place, but it is not our destiny. We are to look for the New or Heavenly Jerusalem. Abraham and Sarah walked with God without a written code to obey. But the laws of God were engraved on their hearts. In the same way, we walk before God, not as the Jew who is obsessed with a written code, but like Abraham, assured that sins are forgiven and we are accepted of God.[24]

It became clear that these people would have to travel a long and arduous road before they were ready to become the 'Holy Nation.' But when they finally entered the land of Canaan as a unified people, with laws, language, customs and a system of religion, under leadership of Joshua, they were ready to possess the land in which God would perform the works that would lead to World

---

Genesis 33: 19.
[24] Romans 4; 13-25.

Redemption. In this Land the Prophets would speak, miracles would take place, and eventually the Son of God would become man. Jesus lived, died, was buried and rose again from the dead in this land. One day, still to come, Jesus will return to this land to establish His Kingdom on earth.[25]

Abraham's role, like his son Isaac and grandson Jacob, was called to '*Sanctify*' the land, setting it apart for the purposes of God, and breaking the curse over it that had transpired through the sin of Ham.

> *Abraham passed through the land to the place of Shechem....then the Lord appeared to Abram and said, 'to your descendants I will give this land.' And there he built an altar to the Lord. Genesis 12: 6 -7.*

Abraham gathered stones from this land and instead of building cities with them, he built altars. Abraham travelled southwards through this hostile arid land until he came to Shechem There he sanctified the land by building his first altar and offering a sacrifice to the Lord to show that he was totally in agreement with God's purpose and would give his life to bring it pass. This the first act of worship to take place in the Land of Promise, and so, the blood of the sacrifice stained the stones of the land and sealed the promises of God into time and space.

---

[25] Zechariah 14: 3-4

Shechem.

It seems that Shechem was as old if not older than Ur. Although an important settlement, it was not as affluent as Ur. Whether or not Shechem had a spiritual significance before Abraham came, is not known for certain, but it certainly did afterwards. Jacob purchased land and dug a well there,[26] Joshua renewed the Covenant here,[27] and Joseph was buried there.[28] It seems that Abraham and Sarah went deliberately to this place and did not come it across accidentally. To be precise, Abraham did not go into the city but camped at the Oak Tree of Moreh on the outskirts of the settlement.[29]

Shechem was situated in more or less the centre of what would become Israel. This could have been significant for Abraham and Sarah. It was, along with the cities Hebron, Ai and Gerar, built at the intersection of major routes of travel. This is why such places frequently occur in the Bible story. To get anywhere you need to pass through them. Shechem is situated between the mountains, Ebal and Gerazim, ideal places to view the vast area of the land.

Abraham the Hebrew. Genesis 14: 13.

This the first time in the Bible that the word Hebrew is used. It went on to become the name of a language and the name of a nation. The word means

---

[26] Genesis 33; 18-20; John 4: 6.
[27] Joshua 24: 1.
[28] Joshua 24: 32.
[29] Genesis 12: 6.

'*to have crossed over.*' As far as Abraham and Sarah were concerned it meant, '*they had come from across the river Euphrates.*' It was a term to identify Abraham, and could have been simply rendered as, '*Abraham from the other side.*' Abraham was never known as '*a Chaldean,*' or, '*a Canaanite,*' but always as Abraham the Hebrew.

I would guess that to cross a significant river like the Euphrates in Abraham's day would amount to the same level of risk as crossing an ocean today. Rivers were natural boundaries between people, and to cross them was risky, not only because off the danger of crossing, but what kind of culture you would encounter on the other side. God describes the boundaries of Eden[30] and the Land of Promise in the terms of rivers.[31]

In Joshua's speech in Joshua 24; 1-28, Joshua reminds the people that not only did their forefathers cross the river, but they too had crossed the Red Sea and the Jordan River in order to enter the promised land. This set them all apart as Hebrews.

Furthermore Joshua mentions 3 times the fact that before their forefathers crossed the river they worshipped idols, but once they crossed; they did not. He then goes on to say that as they had now crossed the waters, in effect, 3 times, they must also put away any idols they had, and worship the God of Abraham only. From this we can understand that to be a Hebrew also means to have turned from idols

---

[30] Genesis 2: 10-14.
[31] Genesis 15: 18

to serve the One True God of Abraham , Isaac and Jacob. It was a spiritual crossing as well as a physical one.

The 1st Altar near Shechem: the Altar of No Return. Genesis 12: 7.

Here Abram built his first altar. He worshipped God and God appeared to him. This initial blessing sets the tone for all subsequent one's. The focus is not specifically or exclusively directed at Abraham and Sarah, but to their descendants. The matter of descendants however, does establish again, that their mission was to be a joint venture, descendants did not only concern Abraham. Doubtlessly this was the significance of this place. It was here Abraham first sanctified the land for the purposes God intended to perform here in the future, not only things that would happen in Abraham's lifetime. [32] We can note again, Abraham Although the land was passed from empire to empire, it would always revert back to Jewish ownership, because God gave the land to

---

[32] The significance of Shechem
    i   Jacob built and altar there. Genesis 33:18-20.
    ii   Jacob dug a well here. John 4:6
    iii Jacob buried the idols here. Genesis 35: 2-4.
    iv Joseph was buried here. Joshua 24:32.
    v   Joshua gathered the nation here to re-affirm the covenant. Joshua 24: 25-27
    vi Joshua designated Shechem as city of refuge. Joshua 20: 1-7.
    vii Abimelech assembled his rebel army here. Judges 9:6
    viii The Northern Kingdom separated from Judah here 1 Kings 12: 1.

He was in the shade of the Oak Tree of Moreh, but as God revealed himself he was transported thousands of years down the corridor of time and he foresaw things that were many centuries into his future. That doesn't mean Shechem became Holy Site for evermore, far from it. It was the place of significant encounters with God, but it was also the place of conflict and rebellion. pitched his tent, but built his altar. Abraham was on a pilgrimage that would continue for millennia after his lifetime, but the encounters with God were a permanent seal of the covenant in this land. Abraham. His tent could be moved, but the altars could not.[33]

The second Altar between Bethel and Ai:[34] The Altar in Spiritual conflict. Genesis 12: 8; 13:4.

We must bear in mind that neither Abraham nor his companions wrote the story down. It was written down many years later from an oral history. We also need to bear in mind that Oral History was very reliable, most unlike modern story telling. The accounts were related over and over and were constantly checked for accuracy by those in attendance.

What tended to happen was, that the places were named as they were known at the time of telling or writing, not by the names from the time the events that occurred.[35] Place names may also have

---

[33] Alexander Maclaren (1826-1910)

[34] Genesis 12: 8.

[35] Genesis 13:18; Mamre and Hebron; Genesis 35:6; Luz and Bethel; Genesis 23:2; Kiriath Arbor and Hebron.

changed since the time of writing, making it difficult to precisely locate them today.

Neither Luz or Ai had any significance at the time of Abraham, but they did become significant later on. Luz became Bethel, the House of God,[36] the scene of Jacob's encounter with God, and Ai became the place where Joshua was defeated because of the sin of Achan.[37] As a result Bethel took on the significance of blessing, the divine presence, victory, holiness and affirmation. But at the time of Abraham as the city of Luz, it was a city steeped in idolatry the same as all the other cities. Ai, became synonymous with defeat, divine absence and sin, Luz with deviation or crookedness. This altar tells us that the journey of Abraham and his descendants would be a constant spiritual battle until the redeemer would come. He carved out a little piece of land on a mountain between Luz and Ai where he would establish the principles of the kingdom that was to come as God revealed them to him. Abraham's altar was *'in between'* or *'in the midst of.'* From the altars all around him the cries to Ba'al, Asherah and the other gods would be heard, but at Abraham's altar he called on the name of the One True God. As Abraham created this holy space in the midst of idolatry, so we, on our journey lift up his Holy name in the midst of the idolatry of our day. We become acutely aware, as did Abraham and Sarah, that the kingdom within us is incompatible with the kingdoms around us.

---

[36] Genesis 28: 16-17.
[37] Joshua 7: 1-8:

The 3rd Altar near Hebron: the Altar of Reconciliation. Genesis 13: 18.

This altar was built after two altercations, one between Abraham and Lot and the other between Abraham and God.

Abraham and God. There was a famine in the land, so, instead of trusting God he journeyed into Egypt to escape the trauma. This created a massive problem for Sarah, nearly de-railing the whole plan, which, will be dealt with in detail later on. Before Abraham could put matters right with God another problem breaks out.

Abraham and Lot. Lot had accompanied Abram and Sarai up to this point and he had also accumulated great wealth. The problem was that their herds were so large, the land could not support them both. Abraham solved the problem by allowing Lot to choose in which direction he wanted to go, and he would go the opposite way. So Lot decided to return to city life and made his home on the east of the Jordan river, amongst the cities of Zoar, Sodom and Gomorrah. Clearly the influence of the city caused Lot to lose what faith he had and to return to pagan customs.

Abraham and Sarai occupied the hill country of the northern Negev. When this was all sorted Abraham built his third altar to mark the reconciliation that had transpired. This signified that although at times they would turn their faces either towards Ai or Luz, there would always be a place where man and God could reconcile.

His 4th Altar at Moriah: the Altar of Redemption.[38]

The significance of this altar would cause all the others to pale in to insignificance. Again, Moriah was not a city. It was a place adjacent to Salem, (that is almost certainly Jerusalem) and was situated just to the north of the settlement. Here Abraham built his final altar. The significance of course was that here Abraham believed that the sacrifice would be his son Isaac.

Strangely Abraham did not plead for his sons life as he had done for the degenerate people of Sodom. He had now come to a place of complete trust and obedience.

'We will come back to you!' Abraham was totally convinced that as he and Isaac climbed the mountain, he and Isaac would return. The bible is saying that God will provide an alternative, or Isaac will be raised form the dead. Either way, Isaac would live.

'God will provide the Lamb!' Abraham had been unable to trust God for his safety, or that of Sarah, in the case of Pharaoh[39] and in the case of Abimelech.[40] But now the lesson had been learned. Abraham knew, that God knew what he was doing, and he would no longer interfere with the plan.

---

[38] Genesis 22: 1-14.
[39] Genesis 12: 10-20.
[40] Genesis 20: 1-17.

Abraham did not take a lamb with him. There was no *'plan B'* as in the case of Hagar.

It is a picture of a God who was prepared to send His Son to die for the sins of the world and a picture of the Son who was prepared to come. As much as Isaac was perfectly capable of resisting his father, as he was not a child,[41] so Jesus could have avoided the cross. But He didn't. Jesus offered back to God, in complete submission, a perfect human life in compensation for Adam stealing the life gift in order to fulfil his own desires. And as a result humanity was free to believe.

According to Jewish stories it was not the same for Sarah. Sources say that Sarah was deeply distressed when she saw her husband and son leave for Moriah. She wasn't stupid, she knew what was going on. Then she was so moved when she saw them returning she was overcome with emotion and died at the age of 127 years.[42]

So the intrepid pair journeyed up and down the land leaving behind them permanent memorials to the reason they had come there in the first place.[43] In general it didn't threaten anyone because the people were not aware of the level of faith on which Abraham operated. They had, through their experiences, mapped out the plan of World

---

[41] Sarah was 90 when Isaac was born. She died shortly after the Moriah incident at the age of 127, so making Isaac to be at least 30 Years old.

[42] The Great Test: The Binding of Isaac by Jacob Isaacs.

[43] Genesis 13; 17.

Redemption, the method and means whereby humanity could be reconciled back to God. There is more to talk about but this concludes the significance of the Altars of Abraham.

They firstly declared that there was no going back. They could traverse the land but they must never leave it. Their focus from now on was to be only towards the future, *'the generations to come.'*

They then acknowledged that the journey would be long and arduous. Until the Redeemer came there would be a tug on one side to sin, disobedience, defeat and despair, but at the same time there would be a tug to the presence of God. The goal of the *'City whose builder and maker is God,'* would only be accomplished by overcoming sin and Satan. It was so for them, the Nation of Israel, and for us as believers today. The final destiny of believers is the glorious age to come, as John envisioned, in a city coming down from heaven.[44]

They learned that even though they, at times, would turn to Ai and Luz, and all that they meant, there would always be a place where the repentant heart could be reconciled.

And finally they learned that God was God when they had no understanding of what He was doing. In their minds they could only conceive the most obscure visions of Calvary, but in what they did, they did in obedience, they demonstrated the archetype of sacrifices. They learned God would never fail.

---

[44] Revelation 21: 2.

Isaac learned he would rather die than doubt the Will of God. Sarai learned that she would rather die than doubt the Will of God, and so she died in faith!

3

Sarah: the woman

Sarah enters the Bible story, quite abruptly, in Genesis 11. Our English versions present her at this stage as just another woman, albeit an exceptionally beautiful one, (Genesis 12: 11) that Abraham met somewhere, fell in love and married. It seems at first glance, that she came from his father's family, but where she fitted in is not yet clear.. We do know she was barren, and that they both knew that they could never have children. This is confirmed by Abraham appointing his steward, Eliezar, as his heir.[45] (Genesis 15: 2)

---

[45] ie. unknown to the narrative.

However, as is often the case when trying to unravel the backstory of a Biblical narrative, things are not quite what they seem to be. As we examine the text a little more closely, a light begins to flicker and an amazing woman emerges from the shadows. Most Jewish commentators set the year of her birth as 1803 B.C.[46] The Bible says that she was 65 five years old when she set out for Canaan from Haran; 90 years old when she gave birth to Isaac; and 127 years old when she died. She was one of only a handful of women in the Old Testament to whom God spoke directly,[47] one of only two women mentioned by name in the roll-call of the faithful in Hebrews 11 and the only one whose age at death is recorded.

We need to start with, what many people believe to be, the most uninspired and boring parts of the Bible, the genealogies. Although these sections rarely produce a preachers text, they do help build the backstory to what is going on. The account that first mentions Sarah is found in Genesis 11: 24-32. The central figure here is Abraham's father, Terah. We discovered he lived to a great old age of 205 years. When he was 70 years old he fathered Abram, Nahor and Haran. (Genesis 11: 26) There are a number of questions we need to ask here.

---

[46] Mishnah. But there is no forensic evidence to support this, however, Matthew 1: 17 can be quoted to indicate her birth was in the region of this date.

[47] Eve. Genesis 3:13.

How did Terah father three children in one year? They could have been triplets. They could have been one set of twins and a single birth. Or it may mean that Terah did not father children before he became 70. There is no clear record of triple births in scripture but a disposition to twins was in the family.[48]

I am not dogmatic about how we should interpret the great ages of the people from the period prior to Abraham. Many take it literally, others interpret it as dynastic, and some see it as fictional. I am inclined to take it on face value. When looking at the births and deaths of the people concerned there is a high degree of correlation. This means even if there is an unknown code involved in the recorded numbers it was the same for all of them, meaning the ages' relevance to one another remains constant. It also shows an agreement with Matthews assessment of 3 x 14 generations.[49]

Another indication of cohesion emerges in the case of Isaac and Rebekah. In this case we see that Rebekah is the granddaughter of Abraham's brother Nahor.[50] This correlates with the fact that Abraham did not father Isaac until he was 100 years old. This meant there was an entire potential generation missing from Abrahams lineage, so making his son and his great-niece, a similar age.

---

[48] Genesis 25: 24.
[49] Matthew 1:17.
[50] Genesis 24: 5.

A similar text to the one we are considering here is Genesis 5: 32. Here it says that Noah begat Ham Shem and Japeth, also implying they were born together. However Genesis 10: 21 tells us that Japeth was the elder brother. Genesis 9: 24 tells us that Ham was the youngest. Shem was 100 years old, two years after the flood. Which means he was 98 when the flood ended, and 97 when it began.[51] This means, that as Noah was 600 when the flood came, he was 503 when Shem was born. As Noah began fathering children when he was 500 years old, then Shem was not the eldest. So we conclude the order of Noah's children by age is, Japeth, Shem, Ham.[52]

This information indicates to us that we should read the text we are considering as saying that Terah did not begin to father children until he attained the age of 70. Who then was the oldest of Abraham's brothers, the middle one and the youngest? We have seen from the account of Noah, that the list of brothers is not necessarily according to age but likely to be according to significance in Biblical narrative.

The fact that Abraham is recorded first follows this principle. Haran was married and had three children and died, before Abram and Nahor took wives. Nahor's wife, Milcah was clearly one of Haran's daughters. This implies that Nahor was more compatible in age to Haran's children than to Haran himself, making Haran the eldest.[53] Furthermore,

---

[51] Genesis 11: 10.

[52] Full Bible Timeline .com

[53] Genesis 11: 29

Abraham regards Lot, another of Haran's children, as his brother,[54] although actually he was his uncle. This also suggests that Abraham was closer in age to Lot than he was to Haran. The fact that Abraham had appointed Eliezer of Damascus[55] as his successor also indicates that Lot, his natural successor, was of a similar age, so it would be pointless to name him as they were likely to die in a close time period. Abraham was only 10 years older than Sarah.[56] We can say with some confidence that Abraham and Nahor were a similar age, but Haran was considerably older.

Haran died before his father and before his children were married. It means he died relatively young for the time, leaving three children. Lot was taken into care, and raised, in his grandfathers' home alongside Abraham and Nahor. Nahor married Milcah and they went their own way for a while. They and their descendants return to the narrative in due course.[57]

Iscah.

The odd person out in this whole thing, and the significant person I wish to get to, is Haran's second daughter Iscah. (*Hebrew-Yiscah; English-Jessica.* Genesis 11: 29)

As people are generally mentioned because they have a part in the story, we must ask, who was Iscah

---

[54] Genesis 14:12
[55] Genesis 15: 2
[56] Genesis 17: 1&17
[57] Genesis 24: 1-6.

and why was she important enough to be mentioned, but apparently nothing more said about her? The intriguing proposition has been made from virtually all Rabbinical sources, that Iscah is in fact Sarai/Sarah, the wife of Abraham! [58] According to Abram's confession[59] she was somehow a descendant of his father, and not an outsider to the family

An interesting account is found in a book called 'The Book of Jasher.' Although a book of this name is mentioned in the Bible (Joshua 10: 12-13; 2 Samuel 1: 18-27) the current document is assessed as being no older than the 18th century. There is no provenance of any kind to link the modern book to the one referred to in the Bible. I mention it because its contents have been used to give detail of Terah's family relationships. The book is quoted to indicate Terah had two wives, one was the mother of Abraham, the other of Sarah.[60]

However the Midrash, as recorded in the Talmud,[61] insists that Abraham and Nahor married Haran's daughters, their nieces, Iscah/Sarai and Milcah respectively.

---

[58] See a similar but slightly different interpretation at Bibleinsight.com
[59] Genesis 20: 12.
[60] The Book of Jashar chapters 15&16, and Doctor Alice C Linsley. Just Genesis.
[61] Shalvi-Hyman Encyclopedia of Jewish Women.

Iscah – Sarai – Sarah. Who says so?

The Bible does not say Iscah is Sarai so how can such a thing be determined? The answer is that it cannot be with certainty, but neither is there direct nor circumstantial evidence to say she is not. On the other hand circumstantial evidence makes it extremely likely. It was part of the culture of the time that marriages took place within the families, usually between cousins and their descendants.

Degrees of Consanguinity.

Daughters and sons of full-blood (same parents) or half-blood (one common parent) relationship, seemingly, had not 'married' each other since the flood of Noah. Genesis 4&5 seem to indicate that the children of Adam formed into two clans, the Clan of Cain and the Clan of Seth, so creating two ever widening genetic streams. It is obvious that mating in this period would have involved activity within the boundary of consanguinity. The proximity of these people to creation would indicate that they had few, if any defective genes, and so disorders that may occur today were non-existent. However as time went on, and the human genome deteriorated, the problem of close-blood mating began to appear. Even today a sibling relationship, although universally forbidden, is not guaranteed to produce physical disorders, it just increases the possibility.[62]

---

[62] Floodgates, David Parsons. Dr J Gough, University of Birmingham, England.

The stories of the flood of Noah,[63] and the destruction of Sodom and Gomorrah[64] indicate to us that at the heart of the culture, there had developed a state of total sexual abandon. Certainly, Matthew 24; 38 records the words of Jesus indicating a debauched state of human relationships. As God's solution to these problems was annihilation, not reform, education, nor faith, we can further assume that the human genetic code had become, or was in danger of becoming, somehow, excessively distorted. Presumably, amongst other things, Noah, his wife, his sons and their wives, were not so genetically deformed and so could produce a new humanity. If we assume that these were the only humans on earth immediately after the flood, the narrative tells us that mating would now be according to a much stricter code. This seems to be the norm as we enter the era of Abraham, because, suddenly, the names of wives are included for the first time since Lamech's wives, Adah and Zillah.[65]

The reaction to Lot and his daughters.

The obvious violation of this code was between Lot and his daughters. (Genesis 19: 31-35) As they were surrounded by the utter destruction of their habitat, they believed they were the only survivors on earth and were afraid that the human race would die out, so they decide to take matters into their own hand, according to the morally depraved code of the city

---

[63] Genesis 6: 1-8; Matthew 24: 37-39
[64] Genesis 19: 4-11; Isaiah 3:9; Jeremiah 23:14;
    Luke 17: 28-30.
[65] Genesis 4: 23.

the angels had forcibly removed them from. The blame is squarely placed on Lot. Although the incest was the daughters' idea, he was a willing participant in that he decided to get drunk and abandon his responsibilities. He had earlier been willing to offer his daughters to the depraved men of the city.[66] This indicates the level of immorality Lot has sunken into.

It was this level of promiscuity that was a factor that caused the destruction of Sodom and Gomorrah. The result was that the two nations that came about as a result of this action, Ammon and Moab,[67] would be a thorn in Israel's side for generations. We see that the prophets linked the action of Lot and his daughters with the depravity of Sodom and Gomorrah[68] The prohibition of inter-relationships between Abrahams family and these people was to last for 10 generations. When we come to the story of Ruth, some 400 years later, the restrictions were relaxed.

I think it is sufficiently clear that the complications of close – blood relationships were well understood at the time of Abraham, and they were passed on down the generations, until they were codified by Moses in Leviticus 18: 1-30; 20: 10-21. Interestingly, the reason given for these laws is found in a little phrase, *'near of kin.'* In other words consanguinity was, to some extent, understood at the time, and that these

---

[66] Genesis 19: 8
[67] Genesis 19: 36-38; Deuteronomy 23: 3-6
[68] Zephaniah 2: 8-9.

regulations were seen necessary to protect humanity from genetic degeneration.

Incest remained taboo at the time of David as is described in the case of Amnon and Tamar as recorded in 2 Samuel 13. The only relationships that were approved were those of quarter-blood or less degrees of affinity. The purpose of marrying within quarter blood or less relationships was to preserve the family heritage, and to ensure the wealth and influence of the family remained within the family. This principle is followed for Isaac (Genesis 24: 1-5) and for Jacob. (Genesis 28: 1-2)

We can compare Lot and his daughters to Abraham and Sarah. When Lot and his daughters were in fear of their extinction they took matters into their own hand. Abraham and Sarah had done a similar thing with Hagar. Both events have ended in trouble for the nation of Israel to this day!

We can therefore expect Abraham to have also chosen a wife, or a wife chosen for him, within his wider family, but outside of the full-blood or half-blood categories, as this is exactly what happened with Nahor and Milcah!

My Sister?

Abraham declared on two occasions that Sarai was his sister, we still have to deal with the reasons and implications of that. Sufficient for now is the fact that it happened; once with Pharaoh, (Genesis 12: 10-

14) and once with Abimelech. (Genesis 20:1) Isaac said exactly the same.[69] (Genesis 26: 6-7)

Furthermore when Abimelech challenged Abraham, (Genesis 20:12) Abraham confesses what he said was to some extent true. He says, Sarah was of his father but not of his mother, seemingly making her and Abraham half-sister and brother. The problem here is that as we have seen that half-blood relationships had become as taboo as full-blood relationships. In what sense therefore, was Sarah Abraham's sister? She could not have been closer than quarter-blood, uncle and niece, or one eighth-blood, cousins. The families at the time were the families of the patriarch as long as he was alive, then, the eldest surviving son became the patriarch. While Terah, father of Abraham, Nahor and Haran was alive, all the family were his children, even if they were grandchildren or even great grandchildren. Hence when Terah decided to travel westwards, he took Abraham and his wife, and Lot with him as part of his household. He would also have taken Iscah, but, as this name is not mentioned in the group that set out from Ur, it leads us again to the possibility that Iscah is in fact Sarai.

If Abraham had married Iscah, the daughter of his deceased brother Haran, as Nahor had done with Milcah, he could, according to the parlance of the time, claim Sarai as his sister. They were all raised in the same household and had the same father or

---

[69] Isaac and Rebekah were second cousins. Terah was both Rebekah's great-grandfather and Abraham's grandfather.

grandfather. They were both of Terah, but of different generations and with different mothers. [70]

Perpetuating the name of the deceased.

Another factor to consider is the custom to raise up children of a deceased person, so that their name would not be forgotten in Israel. The principle is explained in some detail in the story of Boaz and Ruth. It is also called here *'an ancient custom.'* (Ruth 4: 7-12. It was eventually codified in the law. (Deuteronomy 25: 5-6)

The above scenario would explain and harmonize all the scripture references and customs of the time, but did it really work out this way? It is from these ancient sources that we can extract information regarding Sarah. It is the Talmud, based on the oral and literary sources we have mentioned, that says quite categorically, that Iscah is Sarai. [71]

The meaning of the names.

To further build up a picture we need to look at the meaning of the names of the females in the progeny of Terah

Milcah. This is the easiest of the names to understand. Milcah is a feminine form of Melek, which is Hebrew for King. Today we would automatically translate it as 'Queen.' However, at the time there was no such designation as Queen. There

---

[70] Hermeneutics, The Stack Exchange online.

[71] BT Sanhedrin 69b. Josephus. The Antiquities of the Jews, chapter 6.

were indeed female rulers around at the time, like *Kubaba* or *Ku Bao,* the Sumerian ruler. (circa 2500 BC) She was referred to in the Cuneiform tablets[72] as 'king' even though she was female. The Sumerian kingdom was the same region in which Ur was situated, the home of Terah. When Haran named his daughter, he would have been well aware of these traditions.

Furthermore such Queens were not necessarily born into royalty or indeed any kind of status at all. Kubaba, mentioned above, is recorded as having been an innkeeper before becoming a king. Their rise to power was always achieved by the abilities they possessed and their accomplishments. So, a person would become King/Queen by the means of extraordinary characteristics, usually prowess in battle, these were seen as Divine gifts, and were much revered at the time.[73] Milcah therefore was seen as a person of dignity and authority within a certain sphere of influence. Indeed, she became the grandmother of Rebekah, wife of Isaac.

Iscah. (*Hebrew Yiskah*) The meaning of this name is not quite so easy to define, mainly because this is

---

[72] These are a collection of clay tablets that create a narrative of the ancient middle east. Originating in Ur, long before Abraham, Cuneiform script is one of the earliest written languages, with which Abraham and Sarah would have been familiar. Cuneiform means wedge-shaped. The wedge-shaped impression in clay did not represent letters but words and` syllables of words. It was only deciphered in the 19th century.

[73] WWW. Worldhistory.org.

the only time it occurs as a feminine noun in the Bible, and it appears there are no descriptions of the person concerned. The consensus of opinion seems to settle on the meaning, *'To look out as a guard, or look beyond as a seer.'* As biblical names usually described characteristics of the person, we can deduce that Iscah possessed considerable foresight, if not prophetic ability.[74]

Sarai. The consensus of the meaning of this word is, *'My princess, or lady of nobility.'* As such, it gives a hint that it was more of a name of affection from one person to another, and maybe, not a formal name at all.

Sarah. This name also refers to the meaning of 'Princess.' The rabbi's see all kinds of significance in this name change. They see it as an elevation from *'my princess,'* which described her relationship to Abraham, to a *'universal princess,'* a designation God gave her.[75]

However, it is important again we understand that the word *'Princess,'* like the word *'Queen'* are words imposed on the ancient text in an attempt to clarify the meaning to the modern mind. This is called 'dynamic' translation, and seeks to find a modern word that resembles, as close as possible, the

---

[74] Abarim Communications online. According to the Midrash all the Patriarchs and Matriarchs were 'prophets' *Olam Rabbah* 21. The Babylonian Talmud records that God designated Sarah as a prophet in Gen. 21:12

---

[75] Tosefta Berakhot. 1: 13.

meaning of ancient word or phrase. It is not necessarily a direct translation. To us today, a princess is usually a daughter or granddaughter of a reigning monarch, simply by being born, or the wife of a prince. But its official use is relatively modern. The earliest use of the word is in the late 14th century and comes from the French, and denotes the consort of a prince. In Great Britain the title for a monarchs daughter was first changed from 'My Lady' to 'Princess' for Anne Stuart (1665-1714) the daughter of James II, (1633-1701) who became Queen Anne. It was only made an official designation for daughters of the monarch by her successor George I. (1660-1727) In Sarah's case her style would have been best understood as '*My noble lady.*'

In the period we are talking about, as we have seen, there was no concept of a 'Queen.' Female rulers were called kings. As late as the 16th century Queen Elizabeth I apparently included these lines in her famous speech at Tilbury in 1588, seeing herself as a female king:

> '*I know I have the body but of a weak, feeble woman; but I have the heart and stomach of a king, and of a king of England too.*' [76]

Abraham is never called a king. But he does accept deference from kings, and in the case of Melchizedek, who was a king, is acknowledged as the superior person. (Genesis 14) He also was a

---

[76] A letter sent from Leonal Sharp to the Duke of Buckingham 1588. British Library.

person of considerable wealth and influence and commanded a large private army.[77] He was a sort of king without an earthly kingdom! [78]The wife of such a man would be a woman of high status, a *Sarai*!

In addition to the status derived from Abraham, Sarah was a person of incredible significance to God in her own right. She was to be the mother of the *'Promised Child'* through whom all the nations of the world would be blessed. As such God raised her status from *'Abraham's Princess'* to *God's Princess,* according to the description above. (Genesis 17: 15-16)

I am therefore inclined to suggest, in line with rabbinical traditions, that her name was indeed Iscah. Sarai was probably a name of endearment bestowed by Abraham, and beyond dispute, Sarah was a title denoting her significance, bestowed by God, when He miraculously reversed her barrenness.

Rabbinical Anecdotes.

It seems that Jewish Commentators deal with Sarah in a similar way that Roman Catholic and Orthodox Commentators deal with the Virgin Mary. She is elevated to the highest point of adoration and is attributed with being the cause of supernatural events. No one can vouch for the historical accuracy of these accounts, but they serve to tell us the esteem in which Sarah has been held for near-enough 4000 years. If the stories are true, then she

---

[77] Genesis 14:14.
[78] Hebrews 11: 10.

was truly an exceptional and Divinely Anointed woman. If they are exaggerations, then it means she was perceived as such an exceptional woman, and a back-story needed to be formulated. Either way, she was, or was regarded as, an extraordinary woman.

Rashi.[79]

Rashi comments that the people did not believe that Sarah was with child because they knew her to be barren. Hence they accused her of adopting a child and calling it her own. To prove that it was a divine miracle, he records that God enabled Sarah to produce so much milk that she was able to feed her son and countless infants around her. Rashi derives his idea from Genesis 17: 15-16. He says that this is a double blessing in that Sarah not only nursed Isaac, but countless babies who became rulers of nations. It is also recorded that when God favoured Sarah, infertile women became pregnant and there were many healings. As a result of this many people began to believe in the God of Abraham.

The Matriarch.

Sarah was the first of the four Matriarchs of Israel. (along with Rebekah, Rachel and Leah) As such she has come to symbolise the dignity of motherhood for the entire world. She, along with Abraham brought gentiles into the belief in One God, and so founded the Jewish nation. This is deduced from Genesis 12:

---

[79] Shlomo Yitzkaki, known as Rashi. 1040-1105. A deeply revered Jewish commentator.

5-6. The people who were with him were the first converts. God provided manna in the Wilderness for the people of Israel because Sarah had provided the unleavened bread for the Angelic Visitors. (Genesis18: 6) It is said that the name Sarah designated her as a ruler over the people of the entire world.[80] The Rabbi's declared that Sarah was among the four most beautiful women in the world,[81] the others being, Rahab,[82] Abigail[83] and Esther.[84] They said that throughout her ninety years of barrenness she was as beautiful as a bride on her wedding day.[85] She was also regarded as extremely hospitable and showed kindness to friend and stranger alike.[86]

> *"And the life of Sarah was one hundred years and twenty years and seven years."*
> *Notice how her age is recorded in a fragmented and repetitive manner.*
> *The Midrash explains: when she was twenty she retained the beauty of a seven-year-old, and when she was one hundred she was as innocent from sin as when she was a twenty-year-old. In a final summation of Sarah's life,*

---

[80] Shalvi/Hyman Encyclopedia of Jewish women

[81] Babylonian Talmud Megillah

[82] Joshua 2: 8-14.

[83] 1 Samuel 25: 3.

[84] Esther 2: 7.

[85] Babylonian Talmud Olam Rabbah also known as 'The Great Order of the World. It contains a record of the

   Jewish people from creation to Alexander the Great.

[86] Shalom Goodman. Chabad,org.

the Torah tells us two things—that she was beautiful, and that she had a flawless character—her two great qualities juxtaposed.[87]

Her daughters.

Whatever we may think of these Jewish sentiments, these thoughts were not far from the mind of Peter when he wrote his letters. He seemed convinced that Sarah was a woman possessed of a radiant spiritual beauty, irrespective of her outward appearance. She needed no expensive adornment to make her attractive, she was irresistibly attractive because of her *gentle and quiet spirit.* Although these words are directed to women, like the verses that are directed to men, they have meaning for everyone.

> *Wives, likewise, be submissive to your own husbands, that even if some do not obey the word, they, without a word, may be won by the conduct of their wives, when they observe your chaste conduct accompanied by fear. Do not let your adornment be merely outward—arranging the hair, wearing gold, or putting on fine apparel— rather let it be the hidden person of the heart, with the incorruptible beauty of a gentle and quiet spirit, which is very precious in the sight of God. For in this manner, in former times, the holy women who trusted in God also adorned*

[87] Rochel Holzkenner co-director of Chabad of Las Olas, Florida. Et al.

themselves, being submissive to their own husbands, as Sarah obeyed Abraham, calling him lord, whose daughters you are if you do good and are not afraid with any terror. 1 Peter 3: 1-6.

Sarah's daughters do not give way to fear.

The word fear can mean, panic; doubt; unbelief; to cower down; to run away. These are our enemies when we choose to walk in the faith of Abraham and Sarah. There will be nothing in our surroundings to encourage us or to assure us that we are doing the right thing. Our world is as opposed to people of faith as Sarah's was. Our ears need to be attuned to the Word of the Lord and our eyes set on the goal of the kingdom to come.

Sarah's daughters do what is right.

They calmly and unwaveringly trusted in the Word of the Lord. The Word of the Lord takes precedence over circumstances, age, health, and ability. Sarah's daughters, by their example draw others into the faith. Sarah is remembered to this day. Her tomb remains in the city of Hebron, where she rests as a physical memorial to God's faithfulness. But to me, importantly, she stands out, not only in the shadows and types of the Old Testament, but also in the reality of the New Testament, as an eternal example to people of faith.

The '*Incorruptible beauty*' of Sarah is highlighted as an example for all women of faith to follow. Adornment is not banned in these verses, but regarded as insignificant in comparison to the inner beauty of a person.

The Rabbis were so extremely reverent about the name Sarah because it was God- given. They decreed that to call her by any other name, or to mispronounce her name, was a breaking of the law.[88] It was only just short of the reverence that is given to the Name of God himself. That confers on her this most extraordinary status.

The nemesis of Sarah's daughters.

Nancy Campbell[89] intriguingly suggests that the nemesis of Sarah is Jezebel[90]. Particularly the reference in 2 Kings 9:30.

> *She put paint on her eyes and adorned her head.*

In order to give an appearance of authority, beauty, and power, she had to adorn herself, in other words there was nothing in her appearance or character that portrayed such things. It was a false impression. It had carried her for a while, but it would not any longer. Sarah's daughters radiate from within. Jezebel was forever pretending to be who she was not. Jezebel gets a mention in Revelation 2:20-23 where she is described as someone who has an opinion about herself. '*She calls herself a prophetess,*' seems to indicate that the point being made was, that the spirit of Jezebel described

---

[88] Jerusalem Talmud Berakhot 1: 6.
[89] Nancy Campbell www.aboverubies.org
[90] Ibid

people pretending to be who they were not. Sarah's daughters will not get it right all the time: Sarah didn't. But the beauty of the inner spirit means God did not reject her. She could be redirected, rescued and revived, and find the pathway of faith once again.

4

Sarah's message to the people of faith.

As we have indicated in this book, Sarah was not simply following the dreams of her husband. She also had a personal faith in what they were going to do together. Hebrews 11: 11 emphatically states that Sarah personally believed in a God who needed no favourable circumstances to accomplish His goals.

*By Faith Sarah **herself** also received strength to conceive seed, and she bore a*

child when she was past the age, because
she judged *Him faithful who had promised.*

Sarah firstly tells us that it is essential for us to have a personal relationship with God, and not just be in the company of people of faith as was the case with Lot. There was the time when Sarah had to speak up against the wishes of Abraham when Hagar needed to be dismissed. She could only do this because of her personal sense of the calling of God and the importance of her child. Her word was confirmed by God. Sarah is personally included when the heavenly visitors ratify the covenant.

Then God said to Abraham, "As for Sarai your wife, you shall not call her name Sarai, but Sarah shall be her name. And I will bless her and also give you a son by her; then I will bless her, and she shall be a mother of nations; kings of peoples shall be from her." Then Abraham fell on his face and laughed, and said in his heart, "Shall a child be born to a man who is one hundred years old? And shall Sarah, who is ninety years old, bear a child?" And Abraham said to God, "Oh, that Ishmael might live before You!" Then God said: "No, Sarah your wife shall bear you a son, and you shall call his name Isaac; I will establish My covenant with him for an everlasting covenant, and with his descendants after him. And as for Ishmael, I have heard you. Behold, I have blessed him, and will make him fruitful, and will multiply him exceedingly. He shall beget twelve princes, and I will make him a great nation. But My covenant I will establish with Isaac, whom Sarah shall bear to you at this set time next year." Then He finished talking with him, and God went up from Abraham. Genesis 17: 15-22.

Everyone in the Bible whom God renames is given a special status in the unfolding of Divine purposes. [91]However, as in all journeys of faith it was not glory - glory, all the way. Abraham and Sarah had made a pact with each other from the moment they left Haran. They agreed they would introduce themselves as brother and sister.[92] Even though this was a wrong decision, it shows they were in agreement about it and it was not just Abraham's idea. Although they demonstrated incredible faith in setting out at all, they felt they needed a *'get out of jail card'* just in case things didn't work out. God used this arrangement to show how successive generations would react to the Covenant. Everything that happened to Abraham and Sarah was a prophetic sign to their descendants. They lived their lives entirely in view of what was to come. This included the times of great faith, and the times of unbelief. This escape clause caused them to develop a fear of situations that in the end did not transpire. This in turn led to decisions that not only put their lives in danger but caused trouble for everyone around them.[93] This was a lesson to them,

---

[91] Besides Abraham and Sarah there are; Jacob to Israel Genesis 35: 9; Solomon to Jedidiah 2 Samuel 12: 24; and Simon to Peter Matthew 16:18. All believers will be renamed in the Coming Kingdom Revelation 3:12.
[92] Genesis 20: 13.
[93] Genesis 12: 17; 20: 3.

and to us all that to mix fear and faith; doubt and confidence, will have disastrous results.

There are three incidents in Sarah's journey that have extraordinary implications. Each one is prophetic and tend to endorse the belief that Sarah was Iscah, the seer.

Sarah in Egypt. Genesis 12: 10-20.

This is the first of three episodes where I see Sarah as a Prophetess. This story is simple enough, but there are varying opinions about what it means. I would like to present this account as the first of two prophetic demonstrations of events yet to come, not in words, but in Sarah's experience. There are several enacted prophecies in scripture. Probably the most well-known is God's instruction to Hosea to marry a harlot and all its ramifications.[94] We are told that such action portrays God's deteriorating relationship with the nation. However it ends in redemption when Hosea purchases his own wife back from slavery.[95] Jeremiah and Ezekiel frequently enact a scene which has prophetic implications.[96] The theme is, that lapses of faith will put the Covenant in danger, but God will remain faithful and deliver His people.

We have noted that the covenant with Abraham and Sarah would only come to fruition with their descendants. Their entire lives were lived with the

---

[94] Hosea 1: 1-5.

[95] Hosea 3: 1-5.

[96] e.g. Jeremiah 32: 6-15; Ezekiel 24: 1-14.

focus on the generations to come, and in particular the Redeemer. Abraham and Sarah therefore were able to gaze down the corridor of time and see events that would unfold. Jesus confirmed this when he said;

> *'Abraham rejoiced to see my day, and he saw it and was glad.'* John 8: 56.

> *'these all died in faith, not having received the promises. But having seen them afar off were assured of them, embraced them and confessed they were strangers and pilgrims on the earth. Hebrews 11: 13*

This verse confirms that it was not Abraham alone that foresaw the future. All the people mentioned in Hebrews chapter 11 did, including Sarah. The account of the events in Egypt has already taken place when God came to Abraham and gave him the explanation of what had transpired.

> *Now when the sun was going down, a deep sleep fell upon Abraham, and behold a horror and a great darkness fell upon him. Then he said to Abraham, 'Know certainly that your descendants will be strangers in a land that is not theirs, and will serve them, and they will afflict them for 400 years. And also the nation whom they serve I will judge; afterward they will come out with great possessions.'* Genesis 15: 12-14.

What was the *'horror (or terror) and great darkness'* that came upon Abraham?

The transformation of the descendants of Jacob from a tribe to a nation, was to be performed in the Ghettoes of Egypt. Much as it is often said, *'the modern state of Israel arose from the ashes of Auschwitz.'*

This, I believe, was the horror that fell upon Abraham. The nation he would father, would not progress along an ever upward pathway, but, as Isaiah put it, some through the waters some through the rivers, and some through the fire![97] The reason for this was that the Redeemer who was to be born would triumph through suffering at the hands of sinful men. It was as if God was explaining what had happened when he and Sarah visited Egypt, and how it would form the cornerstone of the nation yet to be born. Life would immerge from death; strength formed out of weakness; joy from tears; and deliverance from bondage. Abraham dreamed this, or saw a vision of this. Maybe he saw not only the Egyptian exile, but the Babylonian; the Roman; and the Holocaust. We have already noted that Abraham's prophetic eye envisioned the coming of the Redeemer.

Jesus also positions Abraham talking to Lazarus' nemesis in His illustration[98] and making it clear that Lazarus had gained rest through suffering. As the perpetrator of that suffering the man would not find rest. He goes on to say that Moses and all the prophets tell the same story; the transformation from suffering to blessing. Redemption will be achieved

---

[97] Isaiah 43: 2
[98] Luke 16: 19-31

the same way, when one rises from the dead![99] Finally Abraham condemns the rich man because he trusted in his riches and influence and not in the words of the Prophets, who all declared, that Redemption would be entirely a work of God, so that no one could boast of their achievements.

The final terror of the deep darkness that fell on Abraham was that he realised that Sarah had acted out these events through his lapse of faith and how it was God alone who had delivered her. He finally realised just what a precarious position their pact had placed them in. The similarity between this episode and the Exodus, some 500 years later is not difficult to see. The slavery in Egypt and the deliverance from it is celebrated and re-enacted each year in the feast of the Passover.

- Sarah entered Egypt because of famine in Canaan. Abrahams grandson Jacob and his great grandchildren entered Egypt because of famine.
- Pharaoh was afflicted with plagues in order to let Sarah go. At the time of Moses the plagues persuaded a later Pharoah to let the descendants of Jacob go.
- Abraham and Sarah left Egypt with much wealth. At the time of Moses the Egyptians lavished gifts on the Jews as they left.
- Sarah was placed at the mercy of Pharaoh. Both Joseph and Moses were at the mercy of the Pharaohs of their day.
- The presence of Sarah in Pharaoh's household caused him to give them sufficient

---

[99] Ibid

provisions and livestock so that they could return to Canaan, not merely to survive, but to prosper. The presence of Moses in the Pharaohs household enabled him to be the leader he became, and gave him access to Pharaoh, to plead for, and negotiate, the release of his people.

While Sarah was at the mercy of Pharaoh the whole covenant was in jeopardy. Sarah, through her experience, not her words, prophesied the following;

God would keep His promises.
God would take his people through adverse circumstances.
Those that initially cursed them would bless them.
When people become faithless, God will remain faithful.
An escape clause of doubt caused more trouble than it was worth.

Sarah and Abimelech. Genesis 20:1-17.

This story is the second enacted prophecy. There are similarities with the previous episode, but there are also differences. Abraham and Sarah move deep into the Negev desert and settle in the region of Gerar. Gerar later became part of Philistine territory, and is near what today is called Gaza. At the time of Abraham, Abimelech was king of this region. But was included in the region known as Canaan.

Typically of human beings, the lessons learnt in Egypt seem to have been forgotten. Once more Abraham suffers a lapse of faith and places both

Sarah and the Covenant in jeopardy. Like before he is possessed with a fear of what he perceived was going to happen, but in the end did not,[100] and so took the matter of the Covenant into his own hands. We must learn never to try and work out God's plans and purposes according to our own understanding. Our journey is a walk of faith or it is no journey at all.

This event was within the land of Canaan, which Abraham had dedicated to God by means of his altars. The Covenant would be placed in jeopardy in Egypt and it would be placed in jeopardy by a lack of faith, once they had entered the land. In this prophetic enactment, Sarah demonstrated that just because they had entered to the land they could not live as they wished, but were constantly obliged to trust God and obey His word. Failure to heed this prophecy caused the second exile into Babylon. [101]

It is also important to note that Gerar was near to Kadesh.[102] Kadesh was the place where the Joshua's spies were first sent out to investigate the land of Canaan.[103] The result was a lack of faith, ' *We are not able to go up against the people, for they are stronger than we.'* And so they remained in the wilderness around Kadesh for another 38 years.
Jesus made it clear that rejection of the gospel of the Kingdom would result in a further exile and destruction of the Temple and city of Jerusalem.[104]

---

[100] Genesis 20:11.
[101] Jeremiah 25: 1-12.
[102] Genesis 20:1.
[103] Numbers 13: 21-33.
[104] Matthew 24: 2; Luke 19: 43-44.

Faith was required not only for deliverance from a foreign land, but it was also required to remain in the Promised Land. The journeys of the Covenant people, both then and now, require an implicit trust in God who will complete the work that He has begun. We will never end our journey of faith in this life. The destiny is the Kingdom to come. Never should we try and work out the way God will fulfil His promises through our own ingenuity and strength. Never should we think that we have 'arrived.' God did not need the *'she is my sister card.'* He was quite capable of keeping the Covenant through His own strength.

Get rid of the bondwoman. Genesis 21: 8-13.

The third prophetic episode is quite different. It takes place within the compound of Abraham's tents. Finally the Promised child was born. The incident takes place at a great feast that Abraham had called to celebrate the weaning of the child.

Hagar.

The raising of the status of Hagar from slave/bondwoman to secondary wife, was another disastrous decision, but once again it was made jointly.[105] It seems that at the time, both Abraham and Sarah had given up on the unique role Sarah had been given. They had slipped into thinking that as long as Abraham was the father it didn't matter who the mother was. They were to learn that this was not the case.

---

[105] Genesis 16: 2.

And He said, "I will certainly return to you according to the time of life, and behold, Sarah your wife shall have a son." Sarah was listening in the tent door which was behind him. Genesis 18: 9-10

Hagar was Sarah's maid. She was an Egyptian. Rabbinical Commentators seem convinced she was a gift from Pharaoh to Sarah when they left Egypt.[106] We need to point out that there had been considerable tension between Sarah and Hagar since Ishmael was born some 14 years previously.[107] As fertility and childbirth were seen as the favour of God on a woman, Hagar, unwisely, began to rub it in when Ishmael was born and Sarah remained childless. To all intents and purposes Ishmael was to be the next generation to carry the Covenant, so excluding Eliezar of Damascus. Hagar was his mother with all the potential fortune and fame that would bring. The incident with Hagar is another example of trying to do God's work for him and providing a way around Sarah's barrenness. Not only were things difficult between Sarah and Hagar, but it seems that Hagar raised her son to also despise Sarah.

At the feast things come to a head. Sarah sees Ishmael acting improperly towards Isaac. The incident in Genesis is usually translated as Ishmael *'mocking or scoffing'* at Isaac. However the Hebrew text implies that something much more serious was taking place. Paul seems to know this when he writes in Galatians 4: 29, that Ishmael *'persecuted'*

---

[106] Genesis 12:16.
[107] Genesis 16: 4.

Isaac. The word for 'mocking' is used in Genesis 26: 8 to describe Isaac and Rebekah in an (perfectly legitimate) intimate encounter, and in Genesis 39: 14 to describe the utterly false accusation of a sexual advance by Joseph to Potiphar's wife. This leads us to conclude that Ishmael was somehow sexually abusing Isaac!. This brings us to the third, prophetic incident. Immediately Sarah goes to Abraham and says;

> 'Cast out this bondwoman and her son, for the son of this bondwoman shall not be heir with my son.' [108]

The prophetic word.

This reaction makes it clear that what was going on was no innocent game but threatened the well-being of Isaac and the Covenant. This outburst from Sarah to Abraham, telling him what he should do, was quite unprecedented. Never before had a woman brought the word of the Lord. Abraham was reluctant to do anything about it. But then God spoke to Abraham and confirmed that what Sarah had said, was in fact the word of the Lord! This is helpful for us to know that if we receive a prophetical word it is essential to have our own inner witness that it is of God, before action is taken. Never respond to a direction from someone else if you feel a check in your spirit. It may be right, but until you have received assurance about it, lay it to one side.

---

[108] Genesis 21: 10-11.

Her words are so important that Paul uses them to enforce a principle vital to believers of all generations.

It all sounds a bit drastic and an over re-action. But we must consider: that which is natural and that which is spiritual; that which is of human effort and that which is of Divine intervention; that which is earthly and that which is heavenly; that which is unrighteous and that which is holy: cannot live together in the same household. The ungodly will contaminate the holy and that *gentle and quiet spirit* that is very precious to God, is disturbed and contaminated, and the purity of future generations is compromised.

Very simply there are certain things that cannot be part of the lives of people who desire to walk before the Lord in faith.

> *Do not be unequally yoked together with unbelievers. For what fellowship has righteousness with lawlessness? And what communion has light with darkness? And what accord has Christ with Belial? Or what part has a believer with an unbeliever? And what agreement has the temple of God with idols? For you are the temple of the living God. As God has said: "I will dwell in them and walk among them. I will be their God, and they shall be My people." Therefore "Come out from among them and be separate, says the Lord. Do not touch what is unclean, and I will receive you, I will be a*

*Father to you, and you shall be My sons
and daughters, says the LORD Almighty."
2 Corinthians 6: 14-18.*

There was a substitute in the household.

It is so easy to settle for second-best. Something that
looks like God's will but is not.

> *It happened in the fifth year of King
> Rehoboam that Shishak king of Egypt came
> up against Jerusalem. And he took away the
> treasures of the house of the Lord and the
> treasures of the king's house; he took away
> everything. He also took away all the gold
> shields which Solomon had made. Then
> King Rehoboam made bronze shields in their
> place, and committed them to the hands of
> the captains of the guard, who guarded the
> doorway of the king's house. And whenever
> the king entered the house of the Lord, the
> guards carried them, then brought them back
> into the guardroom. 1 Kings 14: 25-28.*

This passage of scripture illustrates to us the danger
of substituting something for the real thing. Solomon
had made golden shields for his army. When
Rehoboam became king he did not take care of the
golden shields and they were lost in battle. In a
carefree way he just made bronze shields in their
place. However, he took more care of the substitute
shields than the golden ones. It is important to note
the primary purpose of these shields. They were not
so much designed as a defensive weapon but for a
shiny surface to reflect sunlight. The idea was that
as the army would line up for battle they would face

the sun and reflect its rays into the eyes of their enemy, thus making it difficult for them to focus. The bronze shields would do the same thing, but not to the same extent. They were substitutes.

So, Ishmael looked like the child of promise, was raised as the child of promise, behaved like the child of promise, believed he was the child of promise; but he was not the child of promise! It is the same with our worship, He requires *a broken spirit and a broken and contrite heart*, so, a heart *that feels guilty because it was found out,* will not do. A God, whose reasonable demand is for us to be *a living sacrifice,* will not be satisfied with a person who '*tries to fit God in when it is convenient.'* Hagar, like all people who gain an elevated position by human effort and not divine appointment, try and assert and defend their status. They constantly feel threatened. And rightly so, because they are in a place that God has not placed them. The people of faith do not need to do this because God will raise them up at the right time. The substitute must be cast out.

There was a usurper in the household.

As the years went by Ishmael began to believe that Abraham's estate was rightfully his and lived accordingly. We can imagine therefore, how Hagar and Ishmael felt when Isaac was born. All their dreams of power, wealth and influence were under threat. The incident between Ishmael and Isaac we have mentioned, indicates that Ishmael took a chance to try and do some harm to Isaac. The descendants of Ishmael continued to do harm to the family of Abraham and Sarah. They were instrumental in trading Joseph as a slave,[109] and they formed a conspiracy against David.[110] Irrespective of the fact that Ishmael became rich and powerful in his own right, and that he joined Isaac for the burial of Abraham, he seemed to hold a grudge and ensured it was passed along the generations.

This is what Sarah discerned in its embryonic state when she spoke her prophetic word to Abraham. Jealousy will contaminate the household of faith. When someone feels they have a divine right to a status or privilege, despises those whom God as appointed to occupy that status, and makes it as difficult as possible for them, there lies the seeds of trouble. It must be cast out.

There was unbelief in the household.

While Hagar and Ishmael were in Abraham's household there was an alternative to the walk of faith. There was always the reminder that if things got difficult, or God did not work to their agenda, there was an alternative. By saying what she did, Sarah was saying that as Isaac came into the world because of Divine intervention, their on-going journey must be on the same basis. Unbelief must be cast out.

I think that we can see, that to call Sarah's outburst, 'prophecy' is no exaggeration.

Her words were few, but profound; simple and far reaching; relevant to her circumstances, and a

---

[109] Genesis 37: 28 & 39:1.
[110] Psalms 83: 5-6.

yardstick with which we can measure the required action of all people of faith for all time.

> *So, then, brethren, we are not children of the bondwoman but children of the free. Galatians 4:31.*

Holiness.

Holiness describes the moral character of God. It describes His essential nature. If a person were to ask, what is God's essential nature, many today would say, love. However in the KJV the word love is mentioned in regard to God 442 times, while holy occurs 611 times, and holiness a further 43 times.

Holiness describes what God likes and what He hates; what He will accept and what He will reject; with whom He can associate with and whom He refuses to associate with. Both the Old and the New Testaments include these solemn words:

> *But as He who called you is Holy; you also be holy in all your conduct. Because it is written, 'be Holy for I am Holy.' Leviticus 19:2; 1 Peter 1:16,*

To put it another way, God is saying, ' *if you want to be in fellowship with me, then you must be morally like me!'*

When Paul writes in Galatians 4, he uses Hagar as a type or representative of the compromised household. Paul concludes his argument emphatically, '*Hagar and her son must go.'*

Sarah

5

The God of Abraham and Sarah.

I am going to begin this chapter by painting a picture in greater detail of the religious systems that were prevalent at the time in which Abraham declared belief in One God. I am doing this to show that Abraham's encounter with God was remarkable and dramatic. Abraham's belief-shift compares with Jonah's encounter and Pauls' Damascus road experience. It ran contrary to hundreds of years of tradition, and in so doing, Abraham and Sarah initially stood alone against a simmering evil entity.

The Idols of Mesopotamia.

We have noted that Mesopotamia was the cradle of civilisation and idolatry. Much evidence has come to light through archaeology, and as a result we now know quite a lot about what was believed and why. There seems to be a two-tier level of idolatry. One was federal and applied to all the communities in a given region, and so we can speak of the Canaanite religion, the other was local, peculiar to one city state, so we can speak of the religion of Ur.

Any occurrence that could not be easily explained was seen as an action of the gods. Any skill a person possessed that was not common, such as, masonry, carpentry and art, were seen as divine gifts from the gods. A phrase that originated in this scenario, and is still commonly used today is, *'that is a gifted person.'* As such it was seen as a Holy Gift to be kept secret, only shared by a few, and passed onto their descendants. These concepts persisted down to the Middle Ages, evident in the Trade Guilds and apprenticeship system of the time. This concept would include the artistic skills of those who manufactured idols. Religious rituals developed around this understanding. Secret societies or even churches that require a secret knowledge or enlightenment to participate are systems based on idolatry.

An idol was based on imagining super-human creatures that possessed many human traits as well as abilities far beyond human capability, especially the ability to transcend space and time. They could be imagined with wings to imply that they can travel anywhere; multiple eyes meaning that could see everything; large or multiple breasts indicating they were the source of life. These perceptions were then represented in an idol form. This means that the idol would be basically humanoid in appearance but with all these kinds of appendages added. This system of religion dominated religious thought for some 2000 years, right down to the late Roman era.

The idols were made by craftsmen, out of wood, clay and stone under the direction of a priest who held the concept in his mind. There was an elaborate ritual, involving animal sacrifice, that transformed the idol from wood or stone to a divine being. These rituals were done to give the idol the power to speak, see, eat and drink. Of most significance was, when the idol was completed, the craftsman would be required to declare under oath that he did not make the idol, but that the god in question had used his hands. This is referred to in various Bible verses, such as, Deuteronomy 28; Isaiah 40: 18-20.

When all was done, the idol would be placed in a shrine and people would venerate it and make sacrifices to it, in order for favourable things to happen to them.

There were thousands of such idols in Mesopotamia at the time of Abraham, and as we have mentioned, Abraham's father was probably much involved in the idol-making business. The idols were generally regarded as unsympathetic and aloof to human needs, and needed to be persuaded or appeased in order to intervene in human affairs. This made idolatry a lucrative business because each time one approached the idol it was going to cost. When things went wrong it was because the gods were angry, either at the community for omitting a certain ritual, or they were at war with one another, causing the domains of the other gods to disfunction. What is known as Greek Mythology describes this scenario in great depth..

The idols can be placed in certain categories:

The Sky gods.

These were concepts of the powers that made the universe as far as they understood it; governed the passing of time and seasons, and caused the sun to rise and set. They were the creator gods, that through one means or another, produced the universe and life. Although they viewed the universe in this way their understanding of the workings of the cosmos was quite remarkable. These gods were generally regarded as unknowable and the supreme beings in the pantheon.

The Earth gods.

These were a group of concepts that had to do with everyday life on earth. They are often thought of as the offspring of the sky gods. They were much closely associated with everyday life, and as such were much more prominent in the minds of the people. They include the following:

The Survival gods.

These had to do with nature. They influenced the seasons, rainfall, and the harvest.

The Protection gods.

These gods specialised in protecting their followers from plague, disease, enemies and natural disasters such as floods.

The Deliverance gods.

These gods were invoked in the aftermath of a disaster and restore some kind of normality.

The Fertility gods.

These gods were of paramount importance. It was very important that the people could reproduce an ever-increasing offspring. As almost everything was done by hand, the more people-the more work could be done and bigger armies could be raised. According to the Biblical narrative infertility in this period was not uncommon and the reversal of barrenness was attributed to Divine intervention. In a similar way the idolators called upon their gods to maintain fertility. Fertility was also essential for the domestic animals for the supply and quality of food. The shrines of the fertility gods were in much demand. This is made clear in the devious actions of Jacob in regard to Laban's herds.[111] What exactly Jacob did, remains a mystery, but he was certainly aware of something that could alter the natural order.

Healing gods.

The healing gods were a family of gods who conferred the knowledge of medicine to the

---

[111] Genesis 30: 37-43.

apothecaries and 'doctors.' Certainly there was a very detailed knowledge of the effects certain herbs and minerals had on the human body, particularly the hallucinogenic ones. The skill in applying the right potion to an ailment was seen as the intervention of the healing gods. Of course these 'medicines' were also used to disable and cause harm to people. Such action was deemed a curse.

'First do no harm' was not yet the apothegm of the healing arts.. No Hippocratic oath yet! Genesis 20: 17 speaks of a remarkable event of healing through the prayers of Abraham to the One True God. This was really very significant. It was really a *'Mount Carmel Moment.'* The question was, is Abraham's God greater than the customary idols? Indeed He was! Abraham brought healing to Abimelech's household without ritual or sacrifice, but simply by asking God in faith.

The idols of Mesopotamia were essentially a cry from the people for gods that understood the human predicament, would come to their aid and would somehow be prepared to walk the human road. It was an admission that in order to cope with life, super-human help was required from time to time. In this sense they were crying out for an Incarnation or a God-man.

The 'Sons of God' Genesis 6; 1-8.

This enigmatic account suggests that what was taking place was wrapped up in the concepts of idolatry. Whoever the *'Sons of God' were*, and whoever *'the daughters of men'* were, it is clear that they were trying to selectively breed a superhumanity, *'men of renown.'* It was an attempt to make *'a god-man; or a giant,'* so amalgamating the powers of the gods and humanity. It involved the most genetically beautiful women and renowned mighty men. However this attempt at eugenics angered God and triggered the judgement of the flood. Idolatry, in a similar way this sought to merge the supernatural and the natural by nefarious means.[112]

The Idols of Canaan.

Canaanite idolatry was similar in structure to the Mesopotamian system. The pre-dominant names of the Canaanites were Ba'al, a war god, and Asherah his 'mother,' a fertility god.. There are many biblical references to them as their dominance would continue for another thousand years or so. The classical confrontation took place long after Abraham and is described in 1 Kings 18. It was when Elijah and the prophets of Ba'al went face to face on Mount Carmel to demonstrate once and for all who was the Only True God. Much can be gleaned about Canaanite Ba'al worship from this passage. Elijah conceded all the advantages to the Ba'al prophets so it could not be said he deceived them in anyway. (1 Kings 18: 20-25) Elijah then gave them the advantage of going first. It is here that we see a description of Ba'al worship. (1 Kings 18: 25-29)

- They *called* upon the name of Ba'al to come to their aid; there was much frantic shouting.
- They went into a *frenzied dance* around the altar to show their enthusiasm. They were

---

[112] David Parsons. Floodgates.

attempting to demonstrate their devotion to the idol so that the god would react favourably.

- They *prophesied,* deceived by the altered consciousness their frenzy had produced, they thought that communication between them and the god was taking place in a similar way that Eve was deceived in to thinking she was talking to an intelligent snake!

- They sacrificed themselves as an offering to show their devotion. (1 Kings 18; 28) The sacrifice of human life to the idol was the ultimate apostacy. God's life gift, which was described as the image of God in humanity was offered to another god!

It is here we get an introduction to the most despicable aspect of Ba'al worship, human sacrifice, and in particular, child sacrifice.

> *When you come into the land which the Lord your God is giving you, you shall not learn to follow the abominations of those nations. There shall not be found among you anyone who makes his son or his daughter pass through the fire, or one who practices witchcraft, or a soothsayer, or one who interprets omens, or a sorcerer, or one who conjures spells, or a medium, or a spiritist, or one who calls up the dead. For all who do these things are an abomination to the Lord, and because of these abominations the Lord your God drives them out from before you. You shall be blameless before the Lord your God. For these nations*

which you will dispossess listened to
soothsayers and diviners; but as for you,
the Lord your God has not appointed such
for you. Deuteronomy 18: 9-14.

At the same time this shows us what God thought of
the Ba'al worship and a description of what was
transpiring. Later on King Ahaz, (2 Chronicles 28: 1-
4) burnt children in the fire, as did Mannaseh. (2
Chronicles 33: 5-6) The Bible identified idol worship
as demon worship, that is taking God's sacred gift of
life and offering it to another deity! . (Leviticus 17:7;
Deuteronomy 32: 16-18 *et al*) Sadly this did not
deter the Israelites from constantly turning to
Canaanite idolatry.

Elijah spoke to them on the terms that they
understood. 'Maybe he is busy; on a journey; maybe
he is sleeping.' We can detect a tinge of irony in
Elijah's words. He is implying that Ba'al could not
pay attention to more than one thing at a time; he
couldn't be in more than one place at a time, and that
he grew weary. But at the end of it all, nothing
happened, No one answered them nor paid any
attention.

Did these idols have any real power? Idolatry is a
combination of sorcery, witchcraft, occult (secret)
knowledge, divination and illusion. We can expect
that sleight of hand and optical deception, as
performed by stage magicians today, was part of the
package. We can also expect that the use of herbs
and minerals, the effects of which were
hallucinogenic, would create an effect that would be
regarded as miraculous. Beyond all this however
there was a dark spiritual power that enslaved its

worshippers with a wide range of psychological disorders. There was no doubt that their incantations had tapped into demonic forces hitherto unknown. An example of this is when the Egyptian magicians copied Moses. Moses was able to turn his rod into a serpent by the [power of God. The magicians were able to do the same. (Exodus 7: 8-13)

This was the world in which God appeared to Abraham. After the death of his father, Abraham became the patriarch of this branch of the family, consisting of at least, himself, Sarah, and Lot. Abraham decided to travel the journey that he and his father Terah originally planned, and which was so much on his heart to do, and entered the land of Canaan from the north. They set out on a journey that would last for the rest of their lives. Of course they stayed in some places for considerable periods of time, but in reality they were constantly on the move.[113]

We have already indicated that the faith of Terah and Abraham were two very different things. They both set out in the right direction, but one was only prepared to go part of the way. Also Lot did not share the same level of faith as Abraham. Although he travelled with Abraham, the entire enterprise was more an adventure to him than a pilgrimage of faith. He was doing no more than holding on to Abraham's coat-tails. There is no record of Lot ever building an altar. He relied on Abraham's faith, intercession and protection to save him from disaster. (Genesis 14: 14; 18; 27-33) It seems he had no personal experience of Abraham's God. From this we learn

---

[113] Hebrews 11: 9.

that there is no such thing as corporate salvation. In other words, simply by associating with people of faith does not mean we are saved. The principle that has passed down the corridors of time is that we must know God personally. On several occasions the people of Jesus' day claimed their spiritual status was secure by natural descent from Abraham. *'We are Abraham's children.'* However Jesus pointed out that simply to be of the right family was not enough. If they were truly Abraham's children they would walk before God as Abraham did.[114]

El Shaddai.

Abraham and Sarah developed their understanding of the One True God through a series of divine encounters and dramatic experiences. They were free to allow God to reveal himself to them because they stayed away from cities where idolatry would be enforced. They knew their God as *'El Shaddai.'* (Genesis 17:1)[115] The phrase, in connection to identifying God, occurs about 40 times in the Hebrew text and is often translated into English as 'Almighty God'. This name has two implied meanings and one specific translation..

It implies the all-powerful *'God- the Almighty One'-* nothing is too hard for Him.
A second implication is *'God of the Mountain-the high God.'* Later this was rendered as *'El Elyon'-* the *Most-High God.* (Genesis 14: 18) This means that El Shaddai is the real and singular 'Sky God,' in that he

---

[114] John 8; 33-47 *et al.*

[115] Unfortunately, most English translations do not use the Hebrew term, replacing it with God Almighty.

is above and beyond all others. He has no companion and is never in need of council or advice, and he has no beginning and no ending.

But the best meaning is most surprising, it derives from the Hebrew word for 'breasts.' Here it speaks of nourishment and reveals '*The All-Sufficient One.*' Genesis 49: 25. In fact Jacob's blessing to Joseph brings together all of these connotations, The Mighty One, the Shepherd, and the Rock or Stone of Israel. Above all else this is the God who revealed himself to Abraham and Sarah and the One they taught diligently to their household. This shows to us that Abraham regarded El Shaddai as the '*earth God as well as the sky God.*' To him they were one and the same.

> *The God of Abraham praise*
> *Who lives enthroned above!*
> *Ancient, of everlasting days*
> *And God of love. Jehovah! great I am*
> *By earth and heaven confest (sic)*
> *I bow and bless the sacred Name*
> *For ever blest.*[116]

When they travelled on dangerous roads, dwelt among hostile people, faced family disputes, were abducted by foreign kings, and eventually gave birth to Isaac: through it all, God was to them; The All-Sufficient One.

The patriarchs, instead of having a different god for different circumstances, believed in one God for all eventualities. They readily brought the name El

---

[116] Thomas Olivers.1725 - 1799. Redemption Hymnal 6.

Shaddai into every part of their lives. It did not only refer to their object of their worship.

The name was invoked to guide Jacob when he was sent to find a wife.[117]

The name was invoked to protect and obtain mercy for Jacob's sons as they travelled to Egypt for food.[118] It shows that El Shaddai was regarded as a personal God, who was willing to be involved in the day to day lives of his people, and not One far off who had to be persuaded to come to their aid. El Shaddai was not a god like the Canaanite gods, who demanded endless sacrifices, was heartless to human need and fought with other gods for dominance, but was someone, unrivalled, who willingly walked with them on their journey. In Abraham's relationship with God, God took the initiative. We see that God appeared to Abraham and spoke to him. Abraham did not have to go looking for God, God came looking for him. We may also see that the favour of God was conferred by a Blessing in His name, not a sacrifice.

El Shaddai was both the Creator and Redeemer. When Abraham said, *'God will provide Himself, the lamb for the burnt offering,'*[119] he spoke in faith. Because of the profundity of what he said, I doubt if he spoke with understanding. Abraham had just declared that God **himself** would ultimately be the sacrifice. On this occasion God sent a ram in His place because this was not the atoning sacrifice, only a sign of it. But this did not detract from the fact

---

[117] Genesis 28: 3.
[118] Genesis 43; 14.
[119] Genesis 22: 8.

that one day He would send His Son, just as Abraham had brought his son on this occasion!

El Shaddai was considered by Jewish commentators as one of the 7 holy names of God, the others being, *Yhwh, I am, Adonai, El, Tzevoat*[120] *and Elohim.* Once they were written down, they could never be erased. The name Yhwh (Yahweh) was considered so sacred that it was never written or even spoken after the Babylonian exile in the 6th century B.C. It was known as the ineffable Name, that is beyond comprehension; and the unpronounceable Name, meaning, not that it *could not* be spoken, but it *must not* be spoken in case it was mis-pronounced. The only one of these names that remains in common use today, is Adonai, (*the Lord)*

God was also beginning to develop the principle in Abraham's and Sarah's hearts that He would always choose insignificant and unlikely people through whom he would perform the acts that would lead to World Redemption, and He would do these works in arid and undesirable places, so that no one could ever deny that Redemption was a work of God or claim credit. This principle is repeated throughout scripture.[121]

> *For the message of the cross is foolishness to those who are perishing, but to us who are being saved it is the power of God. For it is written: "I will destroy the wisdom of the wise, and bring to nothing the understanding of the prudent." Where is the wise? Where is the*

---

[120] The Lord of Hosts
[121] Genesis 29: 31. *et al*

scribe? Where is the disputer of this age? Has not God made foolish the wisdom of this world? For since, in the wisdom of God, the world through wisdom did not know God, it pleased God through the foolishness of the message preached to save those who believe. For Jews request a sign, and Greeks seek after wisdom; but we preach Christ crucified, to the Jews a stumbling block and to the Greeks foolishness, but to those who are called, both Jews and Greeks, Christ the power of God and the wisdom of God. Because the foolishness of God is wiser than men, and the weakness of God is stronger than men. 1 Corinthians 1: 18-25.

Abraham demonstrated this faith a little later when he and Lot needed to part company because the land could not sustain both of them. (Genesis 13: 8-9) Abraham gladly took the more arid hill country while Lot chose the fertile plains of the Jordan valley. Abraham already believed that his God needed no assistance from natural resources in order to bring about His plan and purposes. The work of World Redemption would be a series of miraculous interventions. Sarah came to believe that her barren womb would produce a child as much as Abraham believed the arid hillside would sustain his flocks and herds.

The God of Abraham was specifically the One:

Who gives life to the dead and calls things that do not exist as though they did, who contrary to hope in hope believed, so that he became the father of many nations. Romans 4: 17-18.

'Contrary to hope,' means that Abraham and Sarah knew full-well the circumstances in which they found themselves, and also they knew full well what God had promised. They chose to believe God!

We read much of Abraham's faith, and rightly so, but we also need to focus on Abrahams hope. Each time he went out at night and looked up at the stars of heaven, he saw the faces of his children yet to be born. He saw the same when he saw the sand of the desert.[122] He lived in the hope of the generations to come. He learned not to be perturbed by the present, but rest in the hope of what was to come. This attitude helps us to cope with trauma, distress, opposition and the trials of life.

> *Now faith is the substance of the things hoped for, thew evidence of things not seen. For by it the elders obtained a good report. Hebrews 11: 1.*

> *Now faith brings our hopes into reality and becomes the foundation needed to acquire the things we long for. Passion Translation.*

When we embrace hope we declare we live for a coming kingdom. Things in this life can come crashing down but that should not disturb us because, like Abraham, we look for a better kingdom which humanity neither built nor can destroy.

---

[122] Paul Yonggi Cho. The Fourth Dimension.

Therefore we do not lose heart. Even though our outward man is perishing, yet the inward man is being renewed day by day. For our light affliction, which is but for a moment, is working for us a far more exceeding and eternal weight of glory, while we do not look at the things which are seen, but at the things which are not seen. For the things which are seen are temporary, but the things which are not seen are eternal. 2 Corinthians 4: 16-18.

Abraham and Sarah's God did not need to be assuaged, persuaded, bribed nor satisfied, unlike the idols of his childhood. Abraham's God was pro-active, He worked to a plan, and called individuals to work with Him in His great cause. He was not constrained by the circumstances of the moment. If what He needed did not exist, He called it into being. He was the Creator God; the God of miracles and supreme over all. As spiritual children of Abraham and Sarah, this is our legacy.

The God of Abraham.

*But you are Israel my servant, Jacob whom I have chosen, the descendants of Abraham My **friend**. Isaiah 41: 8.*

It is incredible to understand that the Eternal God, all powerful and most holy, identifies Himself by joining His ineffable Name with the name of a mortal man, and calling that man, *'His friend.'* God is not ashamed to reveal himself as the God of Abraham. The God we need to know is the God that Abraham encountered, and we need to walk before Him as Abraham did. It was this that caused Jesus to react

90

with incredulity when the Jewish leaders claimed to be spiritual descendants of Abraham. *'If you are children of Abraham,'* He said, *'You would do the works of Abraham.'* (John 8:37- 44) Jesus continued to say that if it was ancestry they were claiming they were more akin to the Devil than to Abraham. In a similar way John the baptiser rejected the claims of the Pharisees and Sadducees:

> *But when he saw many of the Pharisees and Sadducees coming to his baptism, he said to them, "Brood of vipers! Who warned you to flee from the wrath to come? Therefore bear fruits worthy of repentance, and do not think to say to ourselves, 'We have Abraham as our father.' For I say to you that God is able to raise up children to Abraham from these stones. Matthew 3: 7-9*

The faith of Abraham and Sarah is woven through the entire bible and is held up to be the ideal standard and the required response to the promises of God.

> *He did not waver at the promise of God through unbelief, but was strengthened in faith, giving glory to God, and being fully convinced that what He had promised He was also able to perform. And therefore "it was accounted to him for righteousness." Now it was not written for his sake alone that it was imputed to him, but also for us. It shall be imputed to us who believe in Him who raised up Jesus our Lord from the dead, who was delivered up because of our offenses,*

and was raised because of our justification.
Romans 4: 20-25.

This name encompasses the Divine names that emerge from this point onwards: *Rohi* – shepherd; *Shammah* - ever present; *Rapha* - healer; *Jireh* - provider; *Shalom* – peace; and of course *Yahweh* – I am who I am.[123] God made it clear to Moses that the one to whom he was speaking - the 'I am,' was the same God of his fathers, Abraham, Isaac, and Jacob. (Exodus 6: 2-4)

> *El-Shaddai, El-Shaddai, El-Elyon na*
> *Adonai, Age to age You're still the same*
> *By the power of the name, El-Shaddai, El-*
> *Shaddai, Erkahmka na Adonai*
> *We will praise and lift You high, El-Shaddai*
>
> *Through Your love and through the ram,*
> *You saved the son of Abraham*
> *Through the power of Your hand, Turned*
> *the sea into dry land*
> *To the outcast on her knees You were the*
> *God who really sees*
> *And by Your might You set Your children*
> *free*[124]

---

[123] Rohi - Psalm 23:1; Shammah – Ezekiel 48: 35; Rapha – Exodus 15: 26; Jireh - Genesis 22: 13-24; Shalom – Judges 6: 24; Yahweh – Exodus 6: 2

[124] It was written by Michael Card and John Thompson, using direct quotes from scripture as their inspiration, and recorded by Card on his 1981 debut album, Legacy. However, the best-known version of the song was by singer Amy Grant, whose rendition was recorded in 1982 on her platinum-certified album Age to Age.

Therefore it is of faith that it might be according to grace, so that the promise might be sure to all the seed, not only to those who are of the law, but also to those who are of the faith of Abraham, who is the father of us all (as it is written, "I have made you a father of many nations") in the presence of Him whom he believed— God, who gives life to the dead and calls those things which do not exist as though they did; who, contrary to hope, in hope believed, so that he became the father of many nations, according to what was spoken, "So shall your descendants be." And not being weak in faith, he did not consider his own body, already dead (since he was about a hundred years old), and the deadness of Sarah's womb. He did not waver at the promise of

This is El Shaddai. What a contrast to the Canaanite and Mesopotamian gods! How courageous were Abraham and Sarah to make this stand and defy hundreds of years of custom. We owe a debt of gratitude to the faithfulness of these two people who have given the world a glimpse of the One True God, the God of Abraham, Isaac and Jacob; the God and Father of our Lord Jesus Christ, and the One we serve today.

6

Sarah our Mother.

Both Catholic and Orthodox Theology elevates the Virgin Mary to the status of *'Mother of the faithful.'* As she was the mother of Our Lord, it is deduced, she is the mother of us all. She is venerated as the Kings mother as a result of a certain understanding of 1 Kings 2: 13-25. In Old Testament times, the person who usually sat next to the king was not the king's wife, because he often had many wives, but the king's mother. Most of the kings of Judah are introduced to us by stating their age when they became king, how long they reigned, whether they were good or evil, and their mothers' name. It becomes clear that the role of Queen Mother was not just a matter of status but carried with it authority and influence. This can be seen in the reign of Asa who had appointed his grandmother as Queen Mother. When she would not follow him in his purge of idolatry she was removed from her office.[125]

As a result, as late as the English Medieval Court, the king's mother was usually the second most powerful person in the land. The irresistible urge to push Mary further and further up the ladder ended with her fulfilling the *'king's mother role,'* which would be well understood in medieval Europe when the process took place. And like Bathsheba in the previous reference, she could petition the king! We cannot deny that Mary is the mother of the King! Quite why these verses are promoted as a basis for Mary's universal motherhood escapes me, as, in the account, her request is denied and the person in question was put to death.

This said, there is nothing at all in the clear statements of the New Testament that grants Mary a heavenly role any more elevated than any other believer who has completed their earthly journey. Contrary to this Galatians 4: 21-31 presents to us Sarah as the Mother figure of all believers.

Why was the book of Galatians written.

Much of the NT is written to show the superiority of the New Covenant through Jesus over the Old Covenant through Moses. This is only to be expected as the early converts were Jews or people

---

125 1 Kings 15: 9-15.

associated with Judaism. However this does not render the Old Covenant as something to be despised. The law is as applicable to believers in Jesus as it is to Jews.

> *Therefore the Law is Holy, and the commandment holy, just and good. Romans 7:12.*

> *Therefore the law was our tutor to bring us to Christ, that we might be justified by faith. But after faith has come, we are no longer under a tutor. Galatians 3: 25.*

Both Covenants have the same goal, which is, that a Holy God can have fellowship with sinful man. They both contained a priesthood, an atoning sacrifice, and required faith. What has changed is the means whereby this can take place. It is no more as a result of obedience to a series of commandments, but faith in the single act of Atonement by Jesus Christ, which fulfilled the entire law, for all believers; for all time. This is seen as the *New and Living Way* created through the death and resurrection of our Lord.[126]

By the time of Jesus the Jewish people had become slavishly bound to the letter of the law. Jesus' outbursts against the law keepers were never against the law itself but the legalistic way it was applied. The law was never a *'blind guide,'* but those

---

[126] Hebrews 10: 19-22.

who enforced were.[127]Paul, mainly, dismantles all the legal requirements of Judaism **as it had become, far beyond the original intentions of God**. There was no longer any faith, repentance, and humility; **the law had become an end in itself.** To meet the need for the assurance on sins forgiven, peace with God, and the infilling of the Holy Spirit something else was required.

From a child I have heard preachers bellow out, '*We are not under law, but under grace,*' to loud amens. But as non-Jews, we were never under the Law of Moses. We have always been under Grace, some taking advantage of it, some rejecting it. When Jesus challenged the ruler who came to Him asking what must be done to inherit eternal life, it reveals the fact that although the man had meticulously kept the law, he did not experience assurance of salvation. '*What must I do to inherit eternal life?*' The goal of the law, the assurance of sins forgiven and peace with God, still eluded him. Jesus' answer says, that assurance of salvation is not a 'tick box' exercise, and all the wealth he had accumulated is not evidence of God's approval.[128] The assurance of salvation is gained by faith in the divine intervention of Jesus Christ.

Each time this subject arises in the teaching of the New Testament it is to deal with some practical issues that Jewish people were encountering in their transition to Christianity. The particular problem with the churches in Galatia, namely the cities of, Pisidian

---

[127] Matthew 23: 16.
[128] Luke 18: 18-23.

Antioch, Iconium, Lystra, Derbe, Perga and Attalia, was two-fold. They were requiring Gentiles who believed, to first become Jews, and only then could they become Christians. And they were insisting that Jews continued to keep the regulations in their entirety, even after they had believed. This what Paul refers to as, *'a different gospel.'* Galatians was probably the first letter Paul wrote and therefore is dealing with what was a very early problem for Jewish believers. They had not yet grasped what Jesus meant when He said;

> *Do not think that I have come to destroy the law or the prophets. I have not come to destroy but fulfil. Matthew 5: 17.*

We can readily see the relevance of these words as addressed to the situation that Paul faced, but what do they have to do with us who have never been constrained by the minutiae of the law of Moses?

The philosophy of Cause and Effect.

The basis of the law of Moses is cause and effect. God said if you do a certain thing in a certain way, this will result in Divine favour, if you don't do this, then the result will be unfavourable. The famous, *'Eye for an eye'* quote implies that a certain action would require an equivalent response. If you do more, God will do more. When we think of this principle in relation to the law, we can see how easily it becomes a millstone around peoples necks, and how difficult it is to lay it aside. It was much easier to reflect on a lifetime of ritual observance as deserving of salvation, than it was to reflect on the work of Another who has obtained salvation on our behalf.

Of course, '*cause and effect*' are a basic principle of life. If we put our hand in the fire it will get burnt: if we eat healthy foods and we will be well-nourished. The principles are ingrained in everything we do. The problem comes when we try to approach God on this basis. If I do this then God is bound to respond in a certain way. **This is spiritual bondage**. This is where it all applies to us. That is the bondage of the Law. We can all too easily fall into this trap. It is evident in insisting, there is only a certain authentic prayer for salvation, or healing; there is only one specific way of worship that is acceptable; and unless these precise patterns are followed it will end in sickness, poverty, and deprivation. If we are not victorious over every problem, free of all sickness, and, most importantly, wealthy, then our faith is insufficient and we are squandering God's provisions. In fact it can reach the point where we don't actually need God; we believe we have cracked the '*faith-code*,' and can apply our privileged knowledge to any situation.

They brought a woman to Jesus, '*She has committed adultery,*' they said. that was the cause of her arrest: the law says she should be stoned, that was the effect. Jesus said, '*let he who is without sin cast the first stone.*' They all left. *Where are your accusers*? Gone. *Go and sin no more.* That is Divine Intervention between cause and effect. The law had it all worked out. The law was incapable of doing anything except put the lady to death. But when

Jesus intervened the result was entirely unexpected. The charges were withdrawn, sins were forgiven and the woman could start life afresh.[129]

The gospel is superior to this philosophy because between the cause and the effect, there is a point of Divine Intervention which cannot be influenced by human activity. This is the Grace of God. The blessings of the New Covenant can only be received by Grace, through Faith. An authentic Christian conversion comes about when all that has been done by the individual, both good and bad, is laid aside, and we proceed only on what God has promised. So a person is never too good to be saved, and never too bad not to be saved. This is Grace as opposed to law.

So we can say with Isaiah, *'though your sins be as scarlet they shall be as wool, though they be red like crimson they shall be as white as snow.* (Isaiah 1: 18)
Or with Paul,' *therefore if anyone is in Christ he is a new creation, old things have passed away and all things have become new. (*2 Cor 5: 17)

This is where Sarah comes in.

The New Testament makes it clear that Abraham is the father of all the people of faith. He was the first to grasp this principle that there could be a divine intervention that would dramatically alter the course

---

[129] John 8: 1-11.

of events, taking people from curses to blessing, sickness to health, failure to favour and barrenness to motherhood, without any human effort at all. Sarah was the one in whose body the actual divine Intervention would be demonstrated. Abraham and Sarah came to be the first people who rejected the conclusion that barrenness equalled childlessness. And they did it by believing the barren womb would bear a child.

Paul now proceeds to use what happened to Hagar as an example of the *'cause and effect'* people, and Sarah as the example of those who rely on Divine Intervention. It is important to note that Abraham is not the prime example because he was involved in both. It is Sarah who singularly stands out as the one who gives birth to all those who solely rely on Divine Intervention.

As great as Abraham's faith was, it is essential to know who our Spiritual Mother is as well.

> *The Scriptures say that Abraham had two sons, one from his slave wife and one from his freeborn wife. The son of the slave wife was born in a human attempt to bring about the fulfilment of God's promise. But the son of the freeborn wife was born as God's own fulfilment of his promise. These two women serve as an illustration of God's two covenants. The first woman, Hagar, represents Mount Sinai where people received the law that enslaved them. And now Jerusalem is just like Mount Sinai in*

Arabia, because she and her children live in slavery to the law. But the other woman, Sarah, represents the heavenly Jerusalem. She is the free woman, and she is our mother. As Isaiah said,
"Rejoice, O childless woman, you who have never given birth! Break into a joyful shout, you who have never been in labour! For the desolate woman now has more children than the woman who lives with her husband!"
And you, dear brothers and sisters, are children of the promise, just like Isaac. But you are now being persecuted by those who want you to keep the law, just as Ishmael, the child born by human effort, persecuted Isaac, the child born by the power of the Spirit.
But what do the Scriptures say about that? "Get rid of the slave and her son, for the son of the slave woman will not share the inheritance with the free woman's son." So, dear brothers and sisters, we are not children of the slave woman; we are children of the free woman. Galatians 4:22-31. NLT

Hagar.

Hagar is referred to as the 'bondwoman.' She was Sarah's slave. Her son, Ishmael, also had a servant status. Hagar represented cause and effect. She gave birth as a result of the biological process. God was not involved.

What happened to Hagar is Mount Sinai in Arabia: which is where she went when she was cast out. This is the place where the law was given some 400 years later. The law was given, not to be and end in itself, but to lead the Jew to Christ, but it became a *'cause and effect'* system of religion. You have to do things; and you never know when you have done enough.

What happened to Hagar is the city of Jerusalem as it was at the time. Jerusalem had now become the place where the law was forever debated, expanded and enforced: the city that had crucified our Lord, and by so doing rejected the act of Divine Intervention.

Those who seek to emulate Hagar's dilemma. Paul implies that all those who seek to please God out of human effort are possessed with the spirit that involved Hagar and so reproduce the same spiritual bondage. Hagar seized her new-found status and was no longer content to be a member of Abraham's household, she wanted to rule it. The tension between her and Sarah came to a head and Hagar ran away. Sarah blames Abraham for showing favour to Hagar which was contrary to the promises they lived by. God tells Hagar to return. In other words she is given a second chance to be a member of the household of promise. Regrettably, she, and later Ishmael, show they are not content with being a part of the household but want to run it. They are then un-ceremonially cast out. God meets with her and grants her a status, but far away from the household of Abraham and Sarah. She and her son could have been part of the plan of World Redemption, but she could not accept the precedence given to the miracle child. That is the problem with the '*cause and effect*' religion, as soon as things don't seem fair, logical, and predictable, one has to fight to hold on to what was not ours in the first place.[130] There is no place for Divine Intervention. Hagar taught, with catastrophic results, that there was always an alternative to the will of God.

Pauls argument with the Galatian churches was, 'Why would they want to become entangled in this spiritual bondage, when they can enjoy freedom in Christ.' Paul very plainly states that they had been, 'bewitched.'[131]

Sarah. She is referred to as the freewoman. Her identity is linked to the *Jerusalem that is above*. This is the city whose, '*builder and maker is God.*' This is what Abraham and Sarah focused on and why they never built an earthly city. This is the kingdom that was to come which was administered not from a mountain or an earthly shrine, but from the throne of God. It's a kingdom based on Divine Intervention. It is where the normal course of events is dependent upon the will of God. Our prayers, worship and adoration are focused there, where our Lord is seated on His throne, from where God speaks, and from where the Holy Spirit is poured out. It was the object of John's vision:

---

[130] Genesis 16: 1-15.
[131] Galatians 3:1.

But I saw no temple in it, for the Lord God Almighty and the Lamb are its temple. The city had no need of the sun or of the moon to shine in it, for the glory of God illuminated it. The Lamb is its light. And the nations of those who are saved shall walk in its light, and the kings of the earth bring their glory and honour into it. Its gates shall not be shut at all by day (there shall be no night there). And they shall bring the glory and the honour of the nations into it. But there shall by no means enter it anything that defiles, or causes an abomination or a lie, but only those who are written in the Lamb's Book of Life. Revelation 21: 22-27.

Sarah taught that we can rely on the promises of God, and whatever the delay, He will bring it to pass in His time. For a meaningful relationship with God we need divine intervention; a touch of the miraculous; a conversion, a transformation, a heavenly experience, a visitation from above.

The three monotheistic religions, Judaism, Christianity and Islam are all children of Abraham, either biologically or spiritually. All shades of Christianity: Pentecostal, Reformed, Anglican, Catholic, Orthodox, Jehovah's Witnesses, Mormons, whoever, are all children of Abraham, because, no matter how simple, complex or distorted the views may be, they have attempted, one way or another, to place faith in the God of Abraham. Abraham produced both the spirit of freedom and the spirit of bondage, but Sarah birthed

only the child of promise. The question here is, it is not who our father is, but who is our mother.[132]
We are Children of Abraham!

We have mentioned this a couple of times in this book. The Jewish leaders could not grasp why they needed to repent and approach God any differently to their ancestors. They were saying in effect, '*Our salvation is secure because of the faith of our father.*' Jesus called this state of affairs, 'spiritual blindness.' They believed they were God's people and would remain God's people if they meticulously obeyed the law. But Jesus repeatedly pointed out that unless their faith became like Abraham's faith, they were no more children of God than anyone else.

> '*do not say we have Abraham as our father, for I say unto you that God is able to raise up children to Abraham from these stones. (Matthew 3:9)*

In saying this Matthew implied that God could;

- raise up anyone He chose to be his people
- raise up a people who they despised
- raise up a people who did not share their ancestry
- raise up a people who will know God as Abraham knew him.

---

[132] A quote from John Stott. The message of Galatians.

Despite a thousand years or more of substitutionary sacrifices they were now convinced that their status was dependant on their own effort. No one could come to take their sins away; they were only cancelled by their own effort. Those who worship in spirit and truth are those who have had a divine encounter with the risen Jesus. **It's not about what we have done. but what He has done that matters.** Jeremiah prophesied that the day would come that God would write His laws on our hearts. No longer do we need to calculate the minimum required to please God, or how far can I go before I fall off the salvation cliff, but instead we ask, where is the will of God and what can I do to glorify His name.

> *But the Holy Spirit also witnesses to us; for after He had said before,*
> *"This is the covenant that I will make with them after those days, says the Lord: I will put My laws into their hearts, and in their minds I will write them," then He adds, "Their sins and their lawless deeds I will remember no more." Now where there is remission of these, there is no longer an offering for sin.*
> *Hebrews 10: 15 – 18.*

We are children of promise. We believe we are saved because of the promises of God; we believe we can preach the gospel because of the promise of the Holy Spirit; we live as we live because of the promise of the kingdom to come. This is the point Paul was making, you cannot have the spirit of Hagar and the spirit of Sarah together in the same place. **We either walk a life of faith or we don't walk at all.** We are either a believer because of Divine intervention, or we are not people of faith at all. **Cast out the bondwoman and her son.** The two cannot be combined because the spirit of Hagar will destroy the spirit of Sarah. She will rob you of your peace; joy; experiences with the Holy Spirit; it will make you become **jealous; seeking approval; dedicated to achievement; envious; critical; defiant and blame everyone but yourself,** just as Hagar and Ishmael did.

> *Stand fast therefore in the liberty by which Christ has made us free, and do not be entangled again with a yoke of bondage. Galatians 5: 1.*

This is the liberty by which Christ has made us free. Freedom from the bondage of cause and effect, into the liberty of a God who miraculously intervenes. Revelation 21: 2-5. These are Sarah's children.

Then I, John, saw the holy city, New Jerusalem, coming down out of heaven from God, prepared as a bride adorned for her husband. And I heard a loud voice from heaven saying, "Behold, the tabernacle of God is with men, and He will dwell with them, and they shall be His people. God Himself will be with them and be their God. And God will wipe away every tear from their eyes; there shall be no more death, nor sorrow, nor crying. There shall be no more pain, for the former things have passed away." Then He who sat on the throne said, "Behold, I make all things new." And He said to me, "Write, for these words are true and faithful." Revelation 21: 2-5.

7

Sarah's Legacy

The death of Sarah.

The sad story of Sarah's death and Abraham's response to it, is found in much detail in Genesis 23. In honour of his wife, Abraham purchases a plot of land in Canaan, the only piece of land he ever bought. The significance of what he did has repercussions to the present day.

Initially Abraham only wanted to purchase the cave known as Machpelah, but the owner wouldn't sell it without the accompanying 'field.' Please don't think of this 'field' as a paddock of half an acre. According to the value of land mentioned elsewhere in the

Bible, Abraham purchased the cave and about 30 acres of land.

It cost 400 silver shekels. Of course, this refers to shekels as a unit of weight not currency. It was very literally, pieces of silver, not coins. Astonishingly, it has been calculated that in today's terms it would be equivalent to about $600,000.[133]

Why did Abraham want this specific cave?

The scripture indicates that Abraham was well acquainted with this cave, and that he had surveyed it, and concluded it to be an appropriate place to bury his beloved wife, and later himself and his children. He had also researched who the owner was. This is further confirmed when we see he was prepared to pay any price, no matter how exorbitant. The only explanation that exists, is found in the Midrash. Here it states that when surveying the cave, Abraham discovered its secret. It was the burial place of Adam and Eve who had died some 1000 years beforehand! Now you can make out of that what you wish, but there was something that caused Abraham to reject the burial grounds of the Hittites and choose this 'out of sight' place. The site was also called *Kiryath Arba*[134] which is obviously a later name for the place known also as Mamre and Hebron. Kiryath Arba means '*the town of the four.*' Ancient Jewish commentators see this a reference to the 4 people originally buried there, namely, Adam, Eve, Abraham and Sarah.

---

[133] Robert Stieglitz New York University,
[134] Genesis 23: 2.

The Cave.

Machpelah carries the meaning of '*a double cave.*'
Archaeological research at the tomb of the
Patriarchs in Hebron[135] in the 1960's, has shown that
this is indeed the case and that there is one cave on
the top of another. The lower cave is only accessible
from the one above. This would certainly confirm
Abrahams desire to bury Sarah, '*out of my sight*'[136]
or more specifically, in a secret place.
Archaeological research is severely restricted
because of the ongoing clash between Jewish and
Islamic interests. The brief examination that was
done surreptitiously in the 1960's, revealed that the
lower cave is indeed an ancient burial place, with the
bones of several people still lying there intact. The
oldest artifacts found in the cave dated from the time
of Solomon. To the passing traveller it was merely a
cave, but to the enlightened it was the resting place
of the first woman to believe in miracles. Eventually,
despite Abraham's idea to keep it out of sight, it did
become a place of pilgrimage, and remains so
today.[137]

**Why did Abraham buy the cave when he could
have had it for free?**

Ephron, the owner of the land, was a shrewd
business man. He first of all offers the cave for free,
knowing Abraham would refuse. By refusing
Abraham had declared his intention to buy the land
at any price, so Ephron upped the price and
expanded the contract by insisting he buy the field

---

[135] A huge Islamic/Jewish in Mausoleum in Hebron.
[136] Genesis 23:
[137] The Jewish Virtual Library.org

as well. The purchase was a matter of tenure. If he had taken it for free, others would have been buried there, and he and his descendants would have no right of access.

By purchasing the land, Abraham sealed forever the covenant of God, that the land would be the eternal possession of his descendants. God had taken it from Noah's son Ham and his descendant, Canaan, because of his sin, and transferred it to Shem's descendants, and eventually to Abraham. This was no longer only in prophetic terms, but now, in terms that anyone can understand.[138] By purchasing the cave Abraham anchored the promises of God to the land which would become the place where the Acts of World Redemption would take place, including both the first and second comings of Jesus. The cave would also become the resting place of Isaac and Rebekah, Jacob and Leah.[139] The land would forever be an inspiration in Jewish hearts.

As long as within our hearts
The Jewish soul sings,
As long as forward to the East
To Zion, looks the eye –
Our hope is not yet lost,
It is two thousand years old,
To be a free people in our land
The land of Zion and Jerusalem.[140]

Sarah's body was not taken back to the land of her birth as would have been the usual custom. She was buried in what had been a foreign land up to this

---

[138] Genesis 9: 20-27.

[139] Genesis 49: 29-33.

[140] The Hatikvah, (the hope) the Israeli national anthem.

moment, but from now on it would be the focal point of the hearts of Abraham's descendants. This is seen in Jacob's last wish that he be buried here. It is incredible to see that Joseph and a very large entourage, travelled from Egypt to the cave of Machpelah, buried Jacob and returned to Egypt.[141] Joseph also gained assurance that his body would be exhumed and returned to Canaan when the people were liberated.[142] He was buried in Shechem, approximately 100 years after he died, in a place that Jacob had purchased.[143]

The account of the purchase of this land, had, by the time of Moses, become *'tales around the fireside'* but because there was a piece of real estate in their name, it was seen as a token that God would fulfil all his promises, and that they could return to the land confident in the promises of God. Moses had never seen the land of Canaan, and he never entered it! His first encounter with pharaoh was simply to get better working arrangements for his people. When this did not work he cried out to the Lord. It was then that God described to him the significance of the land of Canaan and that it was rightfully theirs to possess as the inheritance of their fathers. From that moment Moses, against all odds, set as his life's mission, to return the descendants of Jacob to Canaan.[144]

Abraham's purchase also has a parallel story in the book of Jeremiah.[145] The setting was the siege of

---

[141] Genesis 50: 1-14

[142] Genesis 50: 24-26.

[143] Genesis 33: 18-20.

[144] Exodus 6; 2-13.

[145] Jeremiah 32: 6-14.

Jerusalem by the Babylonians in the 6th century B.C. The area of Anathoth was already under enemy occupation but he offered to sell a piece of land to Jeremiah that was located there. Jeremiah's uncle was pulling a fast one. He did not have possession of the land but took Jeremiah's money and ran. It seems that Jeremiah was sold a lemon! But it was not so.

> *"Then I charged Baruch before them, saying, [14] 'Thus says the Lord of hosts, the God of Israel: "Take these deeds, both this purchase deed which is sealed and this deed which is open, and put them in an earthen vessel, that they may last many days." [15] For thus says the Lord of hosts, the God of Israel: "Houses and fields and vineyards shall be possessed again in this land."* Jeremiah 32: 13 -15.

Jeremiah was so convinced that the promises of God concerning the land would enable the people to return and possess it, he purchased the field for the future generations. He gained no benefit from the transaction himself, but those who came to repossess the land did. In the same way, Abraham, with his eye on the heavenly city, purchased the land for the benefit of the generations yet to come. It is interesting to see that both Abraham's and Jeremiah's purchase were officially documented.

Abraham buried Sarah in the certain hope of her resurrection.

As Abraham laid Sarah to rest he was convinced that she would rise again from the dead, a lesson he had learned at Moriah. This was not the end of Sarah,

117

just the end of her earthly journey. She had a place in the Kingdom yet to come, alongside Abraham, Isaac and Jacob, 'God had prepared a city for her.'[146]

Sarah was buried in the land of her hope not the land of her birth.

Sarah died looking forward not backward. There was no hint of the spirit of Orpah, who felt her future was better back in her mother's house in Moab than in the land of promise.[147] Having set out, although there were unnecessary detours, there was no turning back. Her eye was focused on a distant place she could barely imagine, but it would come because of her exemplary faith. What an amazing lesson of faith this is to us.

Sarah was laid in the cave as a guarantee of things to come.

Matthew takes great care to show us, at the beginning of his gospel, that Jesus was descended from Abraham and Sarah. He was to be the Promised Child of whom all other descendants had been types and shadows. God chose to demonstrate the kingdom to come in space and time in this land, through the teaching and miracles of Jesus Christ. When our Lord returns, it will be to the land that Abraham consecrated, and from here he will rule the nations.

---

[146] Hebrews 11;16.
[147] Ruth 1: 14-15.

Sarah's Bequest. Genesis 21: 5-7.

God has made me laugh and all who hear will laugh with me.

When Sarah heard the visitors tell Abraham that she would give birth to a child at the age of 90 years, she laughed, not out loud but quietly in her heart. [148] No one knew of her response. This laugh was probably a sort of *'pull the other leg'* moment? Sarah was shocked when one of the visitors asked why she had laughed. How did he know? Seemingly embarrassed she tried to deny it but the visitor insisted that she did. I think it was then that Sarah realised that this was not a human visitor but the Angel of the Lord and his words were not idle chatter. It was exactly the same response that Abraham gave when he heard the news a little earlier.[149]

What the story is conveying to us is that the birth of Isaac would forever be associated with laughter. In fact the name, Isaac, means laughter. It is implying whenever God fulfils His promises it was a time for great rejoicing.

When Nehemiah and Ezra restored the nation after the Babylonian exile, they read again the Law of Moses. Such was the response of the people to this fulfilment of the Divine promises, that Nehemiah declared the day to be a day of rejoicing. From this incident we get the often - repeated phrase:

---

[148] Genesis 18: 10 – 15.
[149] Genesis 17: 17.

The joy of the Lord is your strength.
Nehemiah 8: 10

That day Sarah had laughed in unbelief but she would laugh again out of sheer joy when the child was born. God would take that secret laughter and turn it into a public expression of great joy and it would then become contagious. Whenever anyone received the fulfilment of the promises of God they would be overwhelmed with joy and laughter. When Mary heard of the promised Saviour she rejoiced, and when Elizabeth gave birth to John not only did Elizabeth rejoice but also everyone around her.[150] This is Sarah's legacy: worship was not only a time of solemn reflection, as important as that is, but it is also a time of rejoicing and laughter. Today we can celebrate, and laugh in the goodness of God. Praise and worship are forever to be the response of our heart .As Job discovered:

> *He will fill your mouth with laughing and your*
> *lips with rejoicing. Job 8:21*

Sarah's tent. Genesis 24: 61-67.

The final scene in the life and times of Sarah, as recorded in the Bible, is in regard to the arrival of Rebekah, Issacs wife. Isaac had clearly been greatly affected by the death of his mother some 3 years previously, whom he revered deeply. The text suggests that Sarah's tent had been preserved as a sort of shrine to her memory. From this we can gain a sense of the significance of Isaac giving Rebekah and her attendants this special place to live.

---

[150] Luke 1: 47; 58.

As Rebekah stepped into the tent of Sarah, the calling of Sarah 'veiled' her life from that moment on. The Bible says that as soon as she saw Isaac she covered herself with a veil. The veil is significant in various ways, but as far as we are concerned here, it was the setting apart of Rebekah into the purposes of God. Like her mother-in-law Sarah, she was exceptionally, naturally, beautiful and possessed of an exceptional personality.[151] But she covered the natural beauty so that all that could be observed was the inner spiritual beauty. This is the same inner beauty that Abraham's servant had seen which confirmed to him that she was the chosen bride for Isaac. It was evidenced when Rebekah not only provided the servant with water, but immediately set about the arduous and difficult task of watering 10 irascible camels.[152]

This *'Elijah/Elisha'* moment of succession was of great comfort and assurance to Isaac. Elisha was covered with the cloak of Elijah; Rebekah with the tent of Sarah, but the meaning is the same, the *'spirit and power'* of the predecessor was passed on. In Sarah's tent, she was to live before God as Sarah had done. She became in every spiritual sense, Sarah's daughter.

Rebekah, like Sarah clung tenaciously to the word God had given her:

> *Isaac was forty years old when he took*
> *Rebekah as wife, the daughter of Bethuel*
> *the Syrian of Padan Aram, the sister of*

---

[151] Genesis 24:16.
[152] Genesis 24;18-21.

Laban the Syrian. Now Isaac pleaded with the Lord for his wife, because she was barren; and the Lord granted his plea, and Rebekah his wife conceived. But the children struggled together within her; and she said, "If all is well, why am I like this?" So she went to inquire of the Lord and the Lord said to her:" Two nations are in your womb, Two peoples shall be separated from your body; One people shall be stronger than the other, And the older shall serve the younger." Genesis 25: 20-23.

Here we can see the same faith as Sarah had shining through. When Abraham was faced with barrenness he came up with the idea of a second wife, When Isaac faced barrenness, he prayed. He was not going down the same route as his father.

Sarah had to hold on to the word of the Lord when Abraham was reluctant to send Hagar and Ishmael away. Rebekah had to hold on to the word of the Lord when Isaac seemed to prefer the principle of primogeniture over the word of the Lord. Rebekah believed that Esau had stolen Jacob's place and it was God's will that Jacob was to be born first and receive the blessing of the covenant. Of course Rebekah was right as Sarah had been before her.

The threefold spirit of Sarah, as defined by her three names, passed to Rebekah. *Iscah*: implies her ability to 'see' or perceive spiritual things. *Sarai:* she was beloved of her husband and shared his status. *Sarah*: she was beloved of God and became a

'*Imma b'Israel,*'[153] a mother of the people of faith. We can learn from this that those nearing the end of their earthly journey are to carefully pass on what they have experienced, and those near the beginning should have the grace to receive it.

> *the mark of an extraordinary woman is not how she rises above the rest, it's how she reaches back to raise up others.*[154]

Although the lessons that Sarah has taught us were repeated in the Bible story many times by notable men and women of God, she remains the first, the archetype and the pathfinder. She laid the stepping stones on which Rebekah and subsequently all others, were to place their feet: worshipping the God who called things that were not as though they were. Another important lesson we can learn from Sarah's death is that this present life only makes sense in the light of the Coming Kingdom. To be able to leave a life of comfort and live for about 100 years in a tent only made sense as Sarah focused on the City of God.

Sarah takes her place at the head of a long line of women in the Biblical narrative who displayed exceptional faith. Among them are; Rahab, Tamar, Ruth, Esther and Mary the Mother of Jesus. As worthy, fearless and faith-filled as these women

---

[153] A Mother in Israel.
[154] *Marriane Stluka*

were, Sarah stands out from them all because she was the first.

> *Many daughters have done well, but you excel them all. Charm is deceitful and beauty is passing, but a woman who fears the Lord; she shall be praised. Proverbs 31: 29-30.*

Other Books by the Author

All available on Amazon

Reasons to Believe

This book is a commentary on the Gospel of John. It is structured around the series of 'sevens' in the Biblical Text. As such it shines fresh light on the ancient text and presents a highly readable devotional source. It emphasises John's own declared intention, 'These things are written so that you may believe.'

The Kingdom Unveiled

This book is a detailed study of the Kingdom of God. It deals with many of the difficult matters that are associated with the concept of the Kingdom. Such as, the origin of the concept; the purpose and meaning of parables; the nature of Satan and evil; the Kingdom and the Church; the kingdom in relation to the Nation of Israel; the kingdom and our understanding of the end of the age; spiritual warfare; and how the teaching of the Kingdom shapes our lives in such matters as being peace-makers, stewards of the things of God; and priests in our communities.

The Grace Space.

This book shows how the Grace of God was understood by those who first heard the Gospel. It then traces the story of how it became corrupted by the introduction of many religious practices that are still common today. It deals extensively with the Reformation and the things it achieved but stopped short of a complete understanding of Grace. It generally leans in the direction of Arminianism. It illuminates the subjects of Divine Sovereignty, Foreknowledge, Election, and Perseverance from this perspective. It includes Biblical accounts of the manifestations of Grace and also scenarios from history where the Grace of God was displayed in all its Magnificent Splendour. It concludes dealing with how Grace should be the dominant factor.

The Bruising of the Christ

The book concentrates on the Sufferings of Christ. It seeks to explain how they were anticipated from the Old Testament, describes the details of the Cross Event, discusses the meaning and application to the people of faith.

The Handmaid of the Lord.

A devotional biography on the life and times of the Virgin Mary revealing her as a truly exceptional person. It is written from a Protestant viewpoint based only on the text of the scriptures, with comments about the traditions that have sprung up over the centuries.

Graham Field

Printed in Great Britain
by Amazon

31141757R00079